FOUND

The Lives of Interesting Cars & How They Were Discovered. A Novel.

By Gregory Long

GREGORY LONG

Copyright @ 2014

All rights reserved

Written, edited, cover design, and all photography by Gregory Long who holds their rights through his fictitious *Rain Pillow Press* imprint. For information about permissions to reproduce anything please email the author at
FoundCarsOfCascadia@gmail.com
All excerpts from other works are owned exclusively by their rights holders.

As this is a work of 'Automotive Historical Fiction' — a term I may have just made-up — a few of the characters and events are based on stories I've heard, or read. I've changed things around to retain privacy. Should anyone find anything at issue please contact me at FoundCarsOfCascadia@gmail.com.

Printed in the United States of America

FOUND

FOUND

Dedicated to:

Adolphe, Alex, Alfredo, André, Ben, Björn, Butzi, Carroll, David, Elon, Enzo, Eric, Ferdinand, Ferry, Giulio, Gordon, Hanns, Hans, Hawley, Henri, Henry, Jean, John, Josef, Lee, Lofty, Malcolm, Maurice, Max, Paul, Philip, Preston, René, Robert, Saturo, Sergio, Ugo, Wilhelm, and Zora.

Your brilliance has made my life richer. Thanks.

GREGORY LONG

FOUND

About the Author:

By the (un)acclaimed (non)best selling author Gregory Long who typically goes by Greg but believes that by simply using the suffix 'ory' adds an air of sophistication that may actually help sell books.
A clutch-less '61 Citroën ID19 given to him by his brother for his 15th birthday started Greg(ory) on his life long journey of loving and appreciating weird and wonderful cars. From TR4's to 911's, from Tatras, to too many Citroëns, Greg's garage has always housed something interesting; and usually in need of repair. And now – given he lives extremely close to a

GREGORY LONG

huge body of fresh water—he wishes he hadn't sold his Fjord Green with Apricot interior Amphicar.

Greg lives in the Pacific Northwest with his lovely wife Cath, and three boys. He—like most people reading this book—lacks garage space.

Found is his first novel.

FOUND

Table of Contents:

1st Gear: Breakfast

2nd Gear: Lives of Interesting Cars:
    1. The Red Head
    2. Pinky
    3. The Wedding
    4. Bear Trap
    5. Edgar's Indecision
    6. Plum Crazy
    7. Refrigerators, Horsemeat, and Tatras

3rd Gear: It's a Beautiful Day for a Tatra Hunt

4th Gear: More Lives of Interesting Cars:
    8. Attempted Murder
    9. The Claimer
    10. Road Chiefing
    11. A True 'Sports' Car
    12. Do They Really Go Up and Down?
    13. The Fire Brigade

5th Gear: Lunch

6th Gear: Even More Lives of Interesting Cars:
    14. Z is for Zagato
    15. Black Sea Road Tripping
    16. Worse Than a Car Crash
    17. Dairy Freeze
    18. The Three-Eyed Wonder
    19. Champagne Expedition
    20. Corvette Convenience

Overdrive: The Garages of Mr. Brant
    1. The Roundhouse
    2. The Crow's Nest
    3. Brantville

GREGORY LONG

FOUND

GREGORY LONG

Note to Reader:

Some of the stories you're about to read may end somewhat abruptly: It's intentional. And hopefully keeps you enticed to the end…

FOUND

1st Gear: Breakfast

Tanner finally came across the old BMW coupe. His friend Connor had mentioned he'd seen it at his doctor's office and noticed a distinguished silver haired gentleman struggling to get out, eventually limping into the clinic. Today it was parked at the Mars Cafe. Tanner, with a touch of nervousness, shuffled in.

There, in the corner, sat what Tanner's wife Paige referred to as a GLOM: a Good Looking Older Man. Luckily he was the only person in the joint except for the staff so he walked right over.

GREGORY LONG

"Excuse me sir, do you own that BMW coupe outside?"

"Maybe, you hit it?"

"No sir. I just love old interesting cars. And that's definitely an old, interesting, car."

"Ok, what model and year is it? If you're correct I'll buy you a cup of coffee," Mr. Brant said in a mock curmudgeonly tone.

"Well, let's see. It's an E9 but specifically it's a 1970 2800CS."

"Excellent. How'd you know?"

"I just looked at the script on the trunk lid. No, not really. I checked to see if it had water squirters on the hood, or hidden in the cowl vent. Sure enough they're hidden so I knew it was a 2800. I then visually checked a rear brake through a wheel and saw it lacked discs confirming it was a 2800CS and not a 3.0. And just guessed on the year: Had to be '68 through '71; and they made most of that model in 1970 so I took an educated guess. And, by the way, its exterior colour is Riviera Blue."

"Sit down."

Mr. Brant asked if he was hungry and, of course, Tanner, being the polite young man he is said, "No thank you sir."

"Come on. I can't eat alone. And what's your name?"

"It's Tanner Hamilton. And yours?"

"Mr. Brant."

"Glad to meet you Mr. Brant."

"Feeling's mutual. So breakfast?"

"OK, twist my rubber arm: I'll have the Hungry Man with Canadian bacon, three over-easy eggs, hash browns, and sourdough toast, with raspberry jam."

"You mean easy-over eggs?"

"No, sir. It just rolls off my tongue as over-easy."

"Thought you weren't hungry," Mr. Brant said as he ordered his favorite, corn beef hash. "You have to be damn careful when you order corn beef hash, you know. Most places serve something that looks, and tastes, like dog food out of a can. All minced up. God, I can't stand that stuff. But then, when the stars align, you get corn beef hash that's the best thing on earth. Really. Next to an enormous bowl of lightly salted and heavily buttered popcorn—made in a proper pot on a proper

FOUND

stove—there's nothing better. Mr. Tasty over there makes a mean hash that's impossible to beat. My wife doesn't even try. Couple of easy-over eggs on top and throw it all on a piece of dark rye toast, add a cup-a-Joe and Bob's your uncle. You can't beat that with a stick at any of those so-called fancy restaurants with the tiny portions that somehow get 'plated' and 'paired'. And don't even get me started on 'reposing' meat after it's fresh and hot off the BBQ."

Tanner got up, walked over to Doris and asked if he could change his order. Mr. Tasty gave a shrug and threw another load of hash on the griddle.

Mr. Brant asked, "What kind of car do you drive anyway?"

And was duly impressed when Tanner said, "A Saab Sonett II."

"Where'd you get it?"

"On BaT."

"Bat?"

"You're kidding me. You don't know what BaT is? Bring a Trailer dot com."

"Tanner, there are far more things I don't know, than I know."

"Oh, it's an awesome site. Basically, I think the story goes that there was a guy who loved to scan Craigslist, eBay, and local ads for interesting cars. He'd send the cool ones he'd found to friends who were looking for vintage rides. And then one day he started a website doing the same thing, and Bring a Trailer was born."

"So he posts cars he finds interesting to everyone now, on the web? How's he make money from that? Or is it just a hobby?" Mr. Brant wondered.

"Started as a hobby and I assume it's now a nice business. Everyone sends him stuff they find and he curates a daily list with cars he likes—and those that he thinks will appeal to the readership. He makes money—as best I can tell—by offering really interesting cars exclusively on his site where he gets a percentage of the sale price. They do auctions now too. It's a really amazing business model. And he does ads for shippers and insurers too. You've got to get on the free email blast."

"Email blasts don't sound very friendly; and everyone

keeps talking about spam, or scam—I'm not sure. Anyway, if you think I'll like it I'll give it a try. So does your Sonett have a V4 or that crazy—I mean wonderful—2-cycle engine?"

"It was upgraded to a V4 years ago. I wish it still had the 2-cycle."

"So, other than chasing down old guys with old cars what do you like to do?" Mr. Brant asked sincerely.

"Well, I'm married to Paige and have two little girls, Savannah, and Hutton, and work at the local newspaper as an editor in the online department."

"What the hell ever happened to names like Cathy, or Susan, or Betty anyway? I don't mean to be rude—and those names are beautiful and all—but why do we have to always change things up like that?"

"My nieces' names are Eloise, Eleanor, and Elspeth."

"Yes, that's more like it. Bit of a mouthful when they're all called for dinner though. So, how's the hash?"

"Delicious, and I'm not just saying that because you said it would be. But, even if I didn't like it, I'd probably say I did. My parents taught me little white lies were OK, sometimes. They never called it lying though. They called it being polite."

"What's your favorite meal, Tanner?"

"Nicely plated small portions of French delicacies paired with a refreshing unoaked chardonnay with a meddling bouquet of blackberries, loam, and frankincense," Tanner said with a smirk.

"Nice try."

"Actually crab. I'll do anything for crab. Crab salad, crab cakes, crab sandwiches and, best of all, fresh cracked crab. And skip the purified butter nonsense. No need for butter. No need for cream and sugar in your coffee either, by the way. And no need for ketchup on your French fries."

"Well, I couldn't agree with you less on all accounts. An American who doesn't like ketchup on his fries, sacrilege!"

"I like vinegar."

"Oh God, Canadian?"

"Guilty as charged. And I actually prefer cheese curds and gravy to vinegar."

"Poutine, right? I've done a lot of skiing in Quebec, mostly Mont-Tremblant. Those things are a heart attack just

FOUND

waiting to happen but at 87, who cares? Next thing I know you'll be asking me to pass you a serviette. Or to borrow a toque. Did you travel around Europe with a Canadian flag stitched to your pack?"

"Not Europe but I did go to Australia and New Zealand for a year, hitching and hostelling around both islands, and up and down the east coast of Aussie."

"I've never been in Australia. Spent a lot of time in New Zealand mind you. New Zealand reminds me so much of around here, topographically, I mean. When I was there it had the feel of England in the 1930s but it was in the '60s. Quaint, and charming. And, yes, with lots of sheep."

"I was there in the early eighties," Tanner said. "Reminds me of hitching in New South Wales with my friend Don. We went through a stretch of the Outback — between Charters Towers and Clemont as I recall and it was stinking hot — I mean hotter than a $2 pistol, hot. We finally got a ride with a trucker who had a trailer full of someone's entire household contents. He said he'd give us a lift if we'd help him unload it. And it was a big trailer. A very big trailer. Don and I looked at each other and said 'sure', we were there for the experience and what option did we have anyway? We'd been standing for hours in the scorching sun: We would have done anything to get in an air-conditioned anything. We jumped in the cab but it too was boiling hot. I asked the driver, 'What's up with the air conditioning, broken?'

"'Nope,' he said, 'works fine but I don't want to die out here'. I couldn't quite understand the logic until he said a few miles further down the road, 'Many a trucker has died back out here when their air conditioner goes kaput; and they have to immediately deal with the heat. The sudden change in temperature kills 'em, cold, so to speak. So I don't use it so I'll survive.' Seemed like flawed logic to me but he was older, much more muscular, and nice enough to have picked us up, so I didn't debate it.

And that reminds me of another part of that adventure — Mr. Brant you aren't nodding off, are you?"

"No, not quite yet. I'm captivated by your air conditioning story. It's such a fascinating area of study, air conditioning is. Perhaps you'll regale me with a tale of furnace filter replacement next?"

"One can only hope," Tanner deadpanned.

"So, back to me... the driver just pulls off the highway in the middle of the night and says, 'bedtime, follow me.' Don and I jumped out expecting to be shot in the temple; and go around the truck as the driver opens the huge side door on the trailer and pulls out a bunch of those thick moving blankets and throws them on the ground. 'I'm sleeping in my sleeper, you two sleep out here under the stars. 'Watch out for dingos and snakes though,' he said with a chuckle.

"As we smoothed out the blankets — close to the truck — I asked Don, 'He's joking, right? He wouldn't put a couple of nice young travellers at risk, would he?'

"'No, he needs us to empty the trailer, remember? He'll just kill us after that.'

"As we laid out under the stars the worry faded away as the night sky was like nothing we'd ever experienced. The closest thing to it was at our cabin but it can't compare to being in the middle of the Outback with any form of light around for hundreds of miles. It was glorious. One of those things I'll never forget."

"I had a similar experience recently at a good friends' place on Hardy Island up over by Powell River in BC. They too are completely off the grid and, one evening last summer, the sky was completely full of sparkling stars — it was almost too much to grasp. The entire Milky Way was as clear as day. Wait, that doesn't make sense. Anyway, one of the most beautiful spectacles this long life has ever observed. But back to food, so what about cheddar cheese on a slice of apple pie?" Mr. Brant asked.

"Well, that's a given. And now I know what I'm having for dessert."

"Who said anything about dessert? And who the hell has dessert with breakfast anyway? Mr. Tasty's made a sizeable portion of corn beef hash for you — you couldn't put away a piece of pie now, could you?"

"I know I could; and I bet you could too. And, no, I'm not sharing one with you."

"Oh I hate when people do that. A piece of pie was made for one. That's how the Good Lord meant it when he

FOUND

created those pie cutters that segment pies into perfect sixths, or is it eights? And I've always been partial to those glass cake stands with the heavy glass bowl on top."

"Like over there with the apple pie under it? How about I pick up the pie?"

"You don't pull coin in my town, son."

"OK, I guess that means you won't let me pay, so... I'll have two dozen pies to take home please."

"Nice try."

Coffee turned into corn beef hash. Corn beef hash turned into apple pie. What the hell, he was having the time of his life and didn't really need to go into the office today anyway. *Working From Home* was a beautiful thing.

"Hey Mr. Brant. Do you know anything about Tatras?"

"Yes, a matter of fact I do: Groundbreaking aerodynamic design starting with the T77 in '34."

"Do you know anything about Tatraplans?"

"It's the 4 cylinder version, smaller fin, no louvers, lots of rear windows. They imported some into Canada back in 1950."

"Well I've met an old guy, well, I mean, an elderly gentleman like you..."

"Did you stalk him as well? Does he have a restraining order out on you by chance?"

"Not yet... he told me about an old Tatraplan that's been sitting forlorn in a blackberry bush for decades and gave me sort-of directions. He said he's not mobile enough to check it out himself so I'm wondering if you'd be interested in going on a Tatra hunt sometime with me?"

"I haven't done anything like that in years. I'd love to."

"I've got next Saturday free, you?"

"Tanner, I'm always free. Can we take your Sonett?"

"Can you get in it, is a more relevant question?"

"Of course I can get in it. The question is, will I ever get out?"

"Pick you up at 10 then?"

As Mr. Brant pulled out his Mont Blanc pen and found a clean napkin he replied, "Sure. Here's my address. Don't be late."

Table of Cars:

1st Gear: Breakfast
- 1970 BMW 2800 CS Coupe
- 1967 Saab Sonett II

2nd Gear: Lives of Interesting Cars:
1 -
2 -
3 -
4 -
5 -
6 -
7 -

3rd Gear: It's a Beautiful Day for a Tatra Hunt

4th Gear: More Lives of Interesting Cars:
8 -
9 -
10 -
11 -
12 -
13 -

5th Gear: Lunch

6th Gear: Even More Lives of Interesting Cars:
14 -
15 -
16 -
17 -
18 -
19 -
20 -

Overdrive: The Garages of Mr. Brant

FOUND

1 - The Roundhouse
2 - The Crow's Nest
3 - Brantville

FOUND

2nd Gear:

Lives of Interesting Cars

FOUND

1. The Red Head

    "Hey, aren't you the guy that was asking about that old Ferrari racecar at our filling station a few years back?"

    "What filling station? And what Ferrari," Geoff asked a little caught off guard.

    "Don't you remember an old beat up Ferrari sitting at a Gulf Station on Beardslee Boulevard in Bothell? Remember, you came in and asked about whether it was for sale?"

    "Oh yes, you told me it wasn't; and wouldn't tell me anything else about it either — especially who the owner was — or why it was there. And how did you remember it was me?"

GREGORY LONG

"I'm good with faces; and, well, you're looking at fast cars at a car show. It's now for sale, if you're still interested," Ken said.

Geoff moved away from gazing at the new Cheetah at the '65 *Seattle International Auto Show* and told the gas station owner, "I am. Still at your shop? I haven't seen it parked outside for a long time."

"Nope, it's in a garage in Lake Forest Park."

"When can I see it?"

"How about next weekend?"

"How about right now?" remembering the time he'd lost out on a very early OSCA when someone scooped in and bought it from under him: the lucky buyer hadn't listened to the seller and just went right over with a fist full of cash. He wouldn't make that mistake twice.

"How about we get Spud Fish & Chips on the way over. I'll buy. I'm much more interested in an old Ferrari than anything new here anyway."

"Cod or halibut?"

"Halibut."

"OK, follow me," Ken said.

Geoff, his wife Gloria, and Ken pulled up to a very nondescript line of garage doors behind an old thirties apartment building. Geoff was tingling. Of course he knew it wasn't 'just' an old Ferrari racecar, it was a Testa Rossa: A 1957 250 Testa Rossa Scaglietti Spyder.

Ken fumbled with the key ring for what felt like an eternity until the large dirt brown padlock clicked and opened. The big door came forward, its springs complaining the entire way.

And there it was.

In boxes.

Lots of old crumbling cardboard and wooden boxes. And, in the back of the garage, what looked to be the frame, wheels, and body panels. Upon closer examination Geoff noticed the left front side was caved in.

But it was still heaven on earth. Gloria just shook her head, "Well, this is a disappointment, let's go, we're late for Connie's birthday party anyway."

FOUND

"Are you kidding? I can put this thing back together far better than all the king's horses and all the king's men. Don't you remember what the JX2 looked like when I got her?"

Ken could just feel a sale coming on: He had a livewire.

"Well, Geoff, it's all there but, as you can clearly see, it was hit at Laguna Seca in 1960 and the crank was broken on impact. We tried to get a replacement but Ferrari wanted close to $5,000 for a new one, close to what the owner paid for the entire car when new. He was done with racing—or, more truthfully, his wife told him he was done with racing—so he traded it to me for an old Aston Martin DB2, storage costs, and a bit of cash. That was around five years ago now."

Geoff's internal calculator was working and quickly figured out he wasn't going to get it cheap. And how would he fix, or find, a crank for a V12?

"OK, I'll bite, how much?"

"Five."

"I'll give you $400 as it's all in boxes and obviously needs tons of work.

"Five thousand, and not a penny less."

"It's not worth anywhere near that much and you know it. It's an almost 10-year-old racecar whose days are long gone. That Cheetah we saw at the show today would outperform it."

"Agreed. But it ain't no 250 Ferrari Testa Rossa Scaglietti Spyder either."

Geoff was a newly married young doctor but he didn't have $5,000 unless they put off buying a house for a few more years.

"Let's go Geoff, I bet Connie's waiting to blow out the candles."

"OK, OK, Ken, what's your bottom dollar. I can't do $5,000 especially in this condition. There's a thousand hours of work here and the crank still needs to be dealt with."

"You're the first one to even know I have it for sale. I'm going to put it in the *Seattle Post Intelligencer* next weekend. Maybe I'll be in the mood to dicker a tiny bit if the ad doesn't find a buyer. But I have a sneaking suspicion there are others, like you, who would snap up a 250 Testa Rossa, no matter what the condition. They only ever made 34 of them."

Geoff knew he was right. He grabbed Ken's number and told him he'd call next week and see if it was still available.

Connie's birthday party came and went. They ended up being late but the six year old couldn't care less as they'd brought her a new Easy-Bake Oven.

Geoff slept little that night. And daydreamed throughout the entire sermon. How could he let that Ferrari slip through his fingers like that OSCA?

After church they went out to lunch and Geoff made a new proposal.

"Gloria, I need that car. I know we can't afford it but a chance like this will never come again."

"Didn't you say that about the Allard?"

"Yes, I might well have. So how about I sell it, we take our down payment savings and offer him $3,500."

"You're really going to sell the Allard? I just don't believe you."

"OK, you're probably right.

"Again."

"So, how about we put off buying a house a bit longer."

"Are you off your rocker? You want us to live in an apartment for who knows how many more years so you can buy another old junky car?"

"It's not just any old junky car."

"I know, it's a Fer-rar-i-Test-a-Rossa."

"Do you know what Testa Rossa means, my love?"

"No, but I think you're going to enlighten me."

"Red head."

Gloria looked down at her long, ginger hair. Geoff smiled a puppy dog smile. "Seems like it's just meant to be, doesn't it?"

"What do I get out of this other than no new house."

"How about you can buy anything you want for the rest of our lives. I can't say anything, or even raise an eyebrow."

Connie immediately said, "OK, deal." And they shook on it.

Geoff couldn't get to the phone fast enough. Ring, no answer. An hour later, same thing. Monday, same thing. Tuesday, same thing. Geoff was worried, very worried. After his night shift in the ER he blasted over to Ken's filling station and

FOUND

there he was, closing up.

"Hey I've been trying to call you but haven't caught you."

"Oh, I'm not home much, should have left you the station's number, I'm always here," Ken lied. He'd purposely let the phone ring, guessing it was probably the young doctor.

"Could I look at the Ferrari one more time?"

"Sure, how about tomorrow, I'm coaching Little League tonight."

Geoff couldn't argue with that.

He arrived in the morning to the parts all laid out around the frame and body panels. And there, in the corner, was another guy bent down picking up one of the 12 pistons.

"My dad raced one of these beasts brand new at Watkins Glen. I remember as a teenager watching him. He loved that thing. It was so loud. And so fast. He smartly never let me drive it but I went in it a few times off the racetrack around our neighborhood. Mom hated that thing. Mom and Dad are gone now and I have an inheritance burning a hole in my pocket. I think part of it should go into this car. It would be a great tribute to my dad."

Geoff panicked. He'd got Gloria's approval, even had cold hard cash in his pockets. Damn!

Ken could sense Geoff's concern and sauntered over, "I told a couple of guys at the station about it and this guy just showed up, I haven't even put it in the *PI* yet."

"OK, I'll give you $3,500. I have cash in my pocket. You have the title, in your name, right?"

"Yes I do but like I said, $5,000, not a penny less."

"But I don't have $5,000."

"Then it looks like I'll be keeping the title. Like I said, I'm in no hurry, I can wait till the cows come home."

Geoff blurted out, "$3,600."

"Hey, Ron, what do you think of those red heads? You know Testa Rossa means red head in Italian, don't you?" Ken bellowed.

"I had no idea, nifty," Ron replied.

Geoff rolled his eyes, "Come on, he doesn't know crap. He'll never get it back together. $3,700 and that's all I've got."

"Ron, those are Borrani 72-spoke wheels. And those tires

still have some nice tread left on them, don't you think?"

"Four grand, and that's my final offer," Geoff blurted.

"I thought you just said you didn't have anymore?" Ken said with a smirk.

With that Geoff took the 35 Benjamin's out of his right pocket, and 5 more from his left; and placed them, one by one, in Ken's hand.

"Come on Ken, I'll even let you drive it when it's all back together." Geoff promptly grabbed Ken's right hand and said, "Deal?"

"OK, OK, you win. Let me find a pen and that pink slip."

Geoff quickly backed his dad's Cameo pickup against the garage and started loading the parts. Ron looked up, "What's goin' on?"

"I just bought it. Snooze you lose."

Ron's face turned to disbelief.

Geoff wanted to get out of there before anyone changed their mind; and get home and try to explain to Gloria why they were even $500 lighter than she thought.

Ken closed the garage door and he and Ron jumped in their Studebaker and off home they went. Ken smiled and said, 'thanks', as he handed his son a crisp $100 bill.

"Snooze you lose."

FOUND

2. Pinky

Pinky has always been referred to as eccentric. Even as a young child she did things other girls didn't: built tree forts with no help from her dad; read chapter books years before she should have been able to; even loved olives and caraway seeds.

By the early sixties Pinky had grown the company's revenues ten-fold in only eight years of finally running the orchard. She deserved a treat. She'd grown up on the farm driving pickup trucks. Everyone drove pickups. Foreign cars were suspect.

But Pinky wanted something different. Something

spectacular.

Last year Pinky and her husband Edward went off to Paris for a much-deserved vacation. The food was different, and glorious. The art, superb. Even their love life improved. The overall feel of Paris was just as she'd dreamt.

And she noticed the cars. More precisely, she noticed the lack of pickups. Not one. But lots of little vans. And strange looking taxis. Especially the one with the front that looked a bit like a frog that, soon enough, she found herself only hailing. They were so unbelievably comfortable. They hissed when she entered, and they hissed when she exited. The seats were more comfortable than her living room couch. Her feet were pampered like no other carpet she'd ever walked on.

Finally she got the nerve to try her high school French and ask what kind of car this was as they lacked distinct identifiers on either the inside or outside: Just a few letters and numbers on the trunk lid of some, and a couple chevrons on them all.

"Madame, it's a Citroën DS, of course," the driver said in a rather snotty tone.

How could she not know what a DS was? The President had a DS. All the President's men drove DS's. The DS was the most comfortable, safest, most innovative car ever launched, and that was over ten years ago back in 1955. The DS *was* France.

For the rest of the week they took one to the Louvre, Versailles, even rented one for a couple days to tour the Champagne region outside of Paris.

Pinky decided there and then she needed one. It was sublimely comfortable, had front wheel drive, and one could magically raise the entire car up with a simple flick of a lever on the floor. So, by day, it could zoom around the farm high on its haunches, and, at night, elegantly whisk her to the opera — if only there was an opera in Chelan.

When they returned she secretly checked out who her local dealer might be and, of course, nothing in her small town, but Seattle wasn't *that* far away. Throwing caution to the wind she took the pickup to the big city and first went to *Automobiles Internationales* at 1124 Pike Street. There, right on the showroom floor sat a beautiful sleek black 1967 DS 21 Pallas with a silver

FOUND

roof and gorgeous tabac leather. The salesman came over and greeted the stunning woman wearing cowboy boots, Levi's, and a short black leather jacket. Not your typical Citroën buyer, Jerry thought to himself.

Pinky sat in the backseat first. Just like when she was in Paris. It seemed even more comfortable, if that was possible, just as Jerry said, "This is our Pallas model, higher level of trim and comfort. And this one has the optional leather upholstery."

As she fumbled with the strange rear door handle Jerry opened the back door as he also opened the front. Pinky sat down, grabbed the one spoke steering wheel, and smiled. She wanted this. No, she needed this.

Jerry asked if she wanted to go for a spin. The demonstrator was already outside so they went for a ride around Capitol Hill. Jerry drove first and she noticed he was changing gears with a wand that sprouted from the top of the steering wheel cowl. Jerry noticed her staring, "Oh, that's Citromatic. You change gears, but there's no clutch pedal. Semi-automatic."

And I didn't think this car could get any weirder, she thought to herself, but was clearly wrong.

"It can drive on just three wheels too, by the way. Not that anyone really needs to do that on a daily basis," Jerry said. "But if you get a flat tire that feature comes in handy as you don't need to jack it up—it does it itself."

At the Water Tower in Volunteer Park they switched drivers. Jerry mentioned that the vast majority of first time Citromatic drivers do a pretty, how shall I say, a rather jerky job of it. And Pinky was clearly part of that majority. So much so she thought the whole procedure was crazy: You have to let the gas pedal off just at the right time and then move this little wand also at exactly the right time, and in exactly the right direction.

She said, "Boy, I'm glad they come in standard shift too."

Jerry thought for a moment before saying, "Well, while most folks are puzzled with it at first, the majority love it after a few hundred miles. It's just part of the car's idiosyncrasies—its vive la différence: It's part of what makes a DS, a DS."

Jerry mentioned a line he used often on test drives: "Don't brutalize the lever." This, he explained, came from a recent *Road & Track* magazine test of the DS. The French Citroën mechanic was taking a journalist for a 'test drive' before *Citroën Cars Corp* lent him a DS for the weekend. The reviewer was doing the usual and 'man handling' the shift lever. "Don't brutalize the lever," he was told.

After her lengthy test flight—where they eventually did a big loop around Lake Washington—they returned and Pinky said, "I'll take it, I mean, I'll take it if I can get a great deal on one."

"If you want to get it cheaper then the best way is to pick it up in Paris, use it in Europe, and we'll ship it back home here for you. It's called European Delivery."

Her mind quickly jumped back to the great food, art, and sex, and said, "I'm interested, how much?"

They went back into the showroom, grabbed the color and interior samples and got back into the backseat of the showroom Pallas. "Most comfortable seats we have," Jerry said, with a smile.

Pinky looked up as a rather wildly dressed man walked by, "Is that who I think it is?"

"Yeah, he loves cars and has a DS in for service; and just ordered a new décapotable. He fell in love with them when he lived in London—just like when you went to Paris."

"Décapotable?"

"Convertible, cabriolet, décapotable, I always get mixed up on what's right."

"I don't remember there being a convertible version."

"Yes, but this is the last year they're importing them to the US. That's why he just ordered one. They're built for Citroën by Henri Chapron in Paris. Chapron use to design and build gorgeous custom-built bodies for all sorts of high-end cars since the 1930's—Delahayes, Delages, Talbots and others, and now they build only about a 100 or so DS convertibles each year for the factory, and a few more of their own design."

"Maybe I should get one instead? Do you have a picture?"

Jerry returned with a glossy brochure, "Only pamphlet we have left."

The photo was of a beautiful French woman wearing a flowing white scarf with an Afghan dog lying across the back

FOUND

seat.

"Wow, the model, the dog, and the car are gorgeous!"

"They're the most expensive version of the DS as they're hand-built: Citroën supplies the frame, drivetrain, entire front body and Chapron builds the doors, roof, much of the interior, and entire rear end. It's $5,872 versus $4,564 for a Pallas with leather. All the convertibles come with leather though as standard and you can choose from hundreds of different paint, roof, and leather combinations."

"What color is *Mr. Experienced* getting?"

"White. White paint, white leather, white roof. He obviously likes white cars."

"Well, I think I need something a little less white. How about one that's just like the brochure? I can get a scarf like that but I'm not likely to let Ember our ranch dog lie down on the back seat."

"That's Rouge Rubis, with black roof, and tan leather."

"Ruby red, perfect," Pinky said. "I was thinking pink but there's no way my husband would get near it."

"Good call," Jerry said confidently.

Spring in Paris was wonderful but so was autumn. Pinky and Edward arrived at de Gaulle airport and Edward smiled as Pinky waited for a DS taxi to appear first in line. But was surprised when she said, 'Citroën. Quai de Javel, s'il vous plaît,' Edward picked up the word Citroën just as Pinky gave him a wink and said, "Just trust me dear."

"You rented a DS?"

"Sort of," she replied.

After too much paperwork and passport checking Yves the Citroën representative took them to a covered area inside the factory. And there she sat, somewhat impatiently, waiting for her new owner.

Edward said, "I have a strong feeling this gorgeous machine might actually be our car."

Pinky winked again as Yves helped her stow their baby blue Samsonites in the trunk. The license plate read 5884 TT75 as it was a US version on tourist plates. Yves showed her how to put the roof down for its first drive. Pinky was shaking a bit as Yves went through all the unmarked switches on the dash and was about to show her how to shift but she cut him short, "I know, I know, don't brutalize the lever." Neither he, nor Edward, knew what she was talking about.

Just before they departed, Pinky remembered what she'd tucked in her handbag for just this occasion: pulling out her brand new *Roues de Canon* by *Caty Latham Hermes* scarf, she wrapped it elegantly around her flowing blonde hair.

By the end of that long day they stopped overnight in Sancerre on their way to Provence and those endless fields of lavender. And vineyards. And wineries. Pinky was comfortable with shifting, braking, and life.

FOUND

3. The Wedding

Hannah and Bruce had been going out since 10th grade when she asked him to Tolo. Bruce begrudgingly said yes, not because he wasn't sweet on her, but he just had a lot of work to do on the MG.

His elder brother Tim had gone off to Europe backpacking and left his ratty MG TC to his friend Stuart for safekeeping. Soon after, the little MG's clutch went, and it was relegated to a friend's backyard. It didn't take long for the neighborhood children to find the perfect plaything. And it also didn't take long for them to forget to put the hood back up, or the tarp back on, each time they drove it to Disneyland.

When Tim arrived home after a year of train travel, living in hostels and too much Retsina, he went to his now ex-friend's friend's house and found the car, in a very sad state. The floor was full of water, engine seized, interior destroyed. And, of course, still a bad clutch.

Bruce's birthday was coming up and Tim asked what he wanted.

"The MG," he said with no hesitation. He'd overheard his brother talking with his dad about what he was going to do with it so this seemed like an opportune time.

"OK, but no more birthday presents for at least a decade."

"Awesome, but what's a decade?" was Tim's quick response.

They corralled their older brother Bob into using his truck to drag it home. All piling into the Austin Gypsy, together with a big thick yellow rope, they were off on a rescue mission. Bruce was happy to sit quietly in the Austin for the trip back while his two older brothers swore loudly at each other while trying to negotiate the route without smashing the TC into the back of the Gypsy. They finally made it home—everything in one piece including the brother's relationship. They quietly pushed it around back under the porch where their mom would rarely see it, and Bruce began work. He would have just 13 months to get it back on the road for the first day of his 16th birthday.

Only five years later Bruce was holding something much different than a birthday card—a telegram he could sense was coming, but certainly didn't want. He just didn't understand why they were fighting this war. And why was he being forced to go. Two kids he knew in his small town of Kirkland never came back. Hannah, his girlfriend—and very soon fiancée—felt the same way. She'd lost her dad in Korea and their family life had, understandably, never been the same.

FOUND

"Let's do it. Let's get married. I mean, *'will you marry me?'*"

"Yes, but…don't you think it's a bit crazy? I love you and all that. I want to marry you and spend the rest of our lives' together but you're leaving for Vietnam in 3 weeks. We don't need to do this right now."

"I need to do this right now. I want to commit to you. I want you to commit to me. I want to know I have a wife, and a life, to come home to."

"OK, Bruce, let's do it."

And there was just one more thing he needed to do…

Bruce was the hardest working teenager anyone had ever seen. He'd started mowing all the neighbors lawns at 12, busboy at 13, grocery-bagger at 14 through 15, and pizza delivery at 16. He never stopped. Grades were good too; and he still had time to play ball at Everest Park and spend quality time with Hannah. Life was good.

After 9 years he'd amassed just enough money to buy a new car if he got a good buck for the MG. And he knew exactly what he wanted ever since March 1961 when he'd first read about one at the Geneva Auto Show: the Jaguar eType FHC complete with plate 9600 HP — it had been etched in his memory ever since. And it had to be brand spanking new.

"Bruce, do you think it's right to marry Hannah now," his mother Marjorie questioned. "She won't get her dream wedding because everything'll be far too rushed. Where's she going to get a dress? Where will you have the reception? Guests need more than two weeks notice honey."

"Well, I guess you're right. We'll just elope."

"Nice try. OK, come hell or high water Gwen and I will make this happen if you two truly want it. But no backing out now, ya hear?"

"Yes, mom. Oh yeah, Dave said we could use his swank house and grounds on Lake Washington for the reception. You know, over on Hunts Point."

"Really, does Doris know? That's a huge commitment Bruce."

"Well maybe you can check with her, mom, you play

bridge with her don't you?"

"Yes, but I can't wait for a week from next Tuesday to ask, we've got to get a move-on if we have any chance of this coming together."

"Well I can't think of anyone better to make it happen," Bruce said.

"You know I won't sleep for 3 weeks now, right?"

"Me neither."

Bruce headed down to British Motor Cars in his trusty MG. Walking in the salesman Nathan said, "You're back. Good to see you. How's the TC?"

"It's great. It'll make a fine trade-in on my new Jag," Bruce said trying to catch him off-guard.

"You've finally squirreled away all that cash? You know most guys that buy them are at least two or three times your age, don't you?"

"Yes I do, but they don't work as hard as I do, or save as much as I do either," he said, cockily. Little did they, or anyone close to him, know that he was also dealing in a popular new pastime called marijuana, which he'd deliver along side his 'special order' pizza.

"You're certainly a one-of-a-kind kid, I'll give you that."

"OK, let's do it. I need a Golden Sand XKE coupe with red leather interior and red carpeting. And chrome wire wheels. Just like the one on the Coke calendar at Foo Hongs down the block. It should come to $5,384 pre-tax and license but I'm sure you'll give me a discount given I'll be a long-term customer," he said in a businessman's tone.

"And I need it in two weeks. I'm getting married and then shipping off to Vietnam. So, yes, I am in a bit of a rush."

Nathan tried to stay calm but couldn't, "What, married, 'nam, and a new XKE in all of two weeks?"

"Well, 13 days and counting."

"Bruce we can't get you that particular Jaguar, that quickly. It takes months. You know that. You know more about them than anyone in this dealership, or the entire state for that matter."

"To be honest I didn't think it was possible; but I still want to order it so it's sitting pretty in my garage when I get

FOUND

home."

"Why don't you just order one when you get back—what if a new model comes out in the meantime; you'll have the old model just collecting dust and depreciating?"

"I don't want any new model no matter what. How could they improve on that car? Just look at those glass-covered headlights, that enormous hood, those toggles, and the world's neatest hatch in the rear. Even Enzo Ferrari said it was the most beautiful car ever made!"

"I know. We all know that. We say it everyday to every prospect that walks in the door. I bet Enzo wishes he never said that."

"Well hello, Bruce, we were getting a little worried—seems like you hadn't dropped in for at least two weeks. Thought you'd come down with the plague or something."

"Very funny Mr. Hutchins. I'm putting an order in for an XKE today so you can't make fun of me anymore."

"You really have that kind of cash?"

"Yes, sir. And I expect exceptional service, Mr. Hutchins, now that I'm actually a client of your fine establishment."

"Very well sir, have a seat. Cigar, my good man?"

Except for when Hannah pushed Bruce off the dock and jumped in after him in her mom's wedding dress, Marjorie and Hannah's mom Gwen pulled off the wedding without a hitch. Mr. Hutchins even joined in by providing the wedding party with a jamboree of new Jaguars: 420 sedans and a bright white eType OTS for the bride and groom.

A week later, there were many more tears of a different type as Bruce boarded a bus for camp and then overseas.

Two months later, Bruce's dad Rex received a call from Mr. Hutchins advising him his son's new Jaguar was sitting in the back of the dealership. They hadn't done a single thing to it—just as Bruce had requested. He wanted to see it exactly how it came from the factory, and off the truck, plastic, dirt, and all.

Rex was a little annoyed he had to ante up one of his two garage spaces for the Jaguar but, well, his son was off helping protect the world from those pesky communists so it was the least he could do. He jacked it up, lowered it gently onto wooden blocks so as to not disturb the dirt, or mar the finish. He then draped it with a few wool blankets; and broke down some big cardboard boxes he gotten from the appliance store and placed them, on edge, all around the Jag: He could just imagine himself accidently hitting it with a shovel, or Marjorie bumping into it with the garbage can.

FOUND

4. Bear Trap

Rarely does someone give you a new car. Especially someone you don't know. But it happened to Carter when he was just 18. Off for his first summer job far away from home between freshman and sophomore year. And 'far away from home' meant the wilds of British Columbia's North-Central Interior area, just outside of Burns Lake.

The BC Forest Service had been doing an inventory of the province's Crown land for years. Starting with horses in the 1940's, men would traipse off into the bush and count trees. The foresters needed to know how many they had, their size,

43

condition, species, and overall health. From those calculations they'd provide appropriate size tree licenses to the logging companies. This was the concept of sustainability long before the word appeared in our lexicon. Trees are a renewable resource but because a seedling takes so long to mature the effort was to ensure the mighty forests of British Columbia stayed mighty.

And counting trees isn't quite as simple as, *'There's one, and another... Oh, hey, look over there, another one, that makes three!'*

Carter was learning the ropes—literally—at *Green Timbers Training Centre* in Surrey before he was sent up north. Learning how to be a Compassman was not that tough in the confines of a classroom but it would be far more difficult going in an unwavering straight line no matter what Devil's Club, Skunk Cabbage, giant boulders, and vertical stream banks were blocking your way. It was imperative you got your Tallyman to the exact spot on the aerial photograph the professional forester had specified from their comfy warm offices in Victoria over the previous winter.

About half way through the first week Carter was presented with a brand new '74 Land Rover 88 Series III. The BCFS had been using Land Rovers for decades as the 'go to' vehicle for traveling the back roads and dirt tracks to ensure Compassmen and Tallymen got as close to their samples as possible. Throughout the late sixties and into the seventies Ford Bronco's and Dodge Power Wagons took some of the spots old Land Rovers were vacating as they aged; this was to be the last year for new Land Rovers because importation to North America had been curtailed.

In the end, however, because they were still the best off-road vehicles, especially for going places no one had been to for years, if ever, each of the half dozen camps strewn across British Columbia were given at least one Rover. Carter was the happy recipient of the truck for Burns Lake Camp, 613 miles north.

Even fresh out of its wrapper it was slow, noisy, and rough riding. Some of the new Bronco's had huge V8's so Carter's journey took a little bit longer. But he didn't care; he was on the clock being paid good money to drive a new truck through, as the license plates say, Beautiful British Columbia.

Sometimes the crew could just jump out of the truck and

FOUND

take the sample but many more times they had to hike to an identifiable spot on the aerial photograph and then use a 200-foot metal measuring tape to land exactly in the middle of the sample they wanted to take. Each time the Tallyman was close to running out of tape they'd yell the word 'poop' which told the 'Compassman' — who was out forging ahead — to get ready to stop. This was called the 'poop chain' and poop was called out because it was easy to hear in the bush. So, yes, students were being well paid to hike and 'poop' though some of the most beautiful scenery in the world.

Sometimes the samples were in areas so remote helicopters were used. However, it was so expensive to commute by chopper they would, on most occasions, drop foresters off in or near a swamp with their gear and pick them up a few days later. Here they would set up camp. Kraft Dinner and tuna would be made for dinner, and the rest of the evening spent swatting giant mosquitoes in the tent before trying to sleep.

Being out in the forest where, in most cases, a human had never set foot, they'd see a lot of wildlife but it was never a problem, except once. It was in the mountains where a rockslide had wiped out an old logging road where Carter and his Compassman were headed. They gathered up their tools of the trade, threw in their packed lunches, and headed out walking to the sample.

It wasn't a normal flat road through the forest; it was literally cut out of a mountain, twisting along between a river far below and sheer cliffs above. Carter had been walking for over a half hour when he saw it. A bear. And not a normal black or brown bear but a HUGE grizzly bear! Coming right towards him. The bear's head was down, just lumbering along. Carter couldn't go up the cliff to his left, or down the cliff to his right. The only place to go was to retrace his tracks back to the truck. Now everything they'd been trained on said not to run.

But he ran.

Fast.

Carter was walking ahead of Gabrielle and when she saw him running back towards her she instinctively turned around, dropped her tally-bag knapsack too and ran beside him asking what was up. Carter said, 'Bear. Grizzly bear.' Gabrielle started running faster. They made it back to the truck in Olympic gold medal time; and evidentially the wind was blowing the other direction and that he mustn't have smelled their scent. Or perhaps he did and had just come across the knapsacks, smelled the lunches, and ate them first. Perhaps their lunches saved their lives?

In the rush Carter had dropped the keys—who could blame him—which he hadn't noticed until they'd reached the Rover. Where was the grizzly? Where are the keys! And why did they lock the stupid thing when they were in the middle of nowhere anyway? Carter smashed the driver's window in before remembering they'd hidden a spare key up under the rear bumper at Green Timbers. He ran around the back, found it, opened the door, swept away the broken glass, and attempted to make a getaway.

But it wouldn't start.

Prince of Darkness? Nope, vapor lock. It had been having problems in hot weather and of course it was happening again; and the driver's window was now wide open as he saw the bear, in the mirror, coming around the bend.

Thankfully they'd done exactly what they'd been trained to do at Green Timbers—turned the truck around 180 degrees before they left on the sample. This was done so that if anyone got hurt they'd save time in turning around—no one ever said anything about an unfriendly confrontation with a massive grizzly.

Carter quickly popped it in neutral, threw the parking brake off, and luckily they were at the top of a long downhill part of the fire road.

When they rolled to a stop at the bottom the bear was nowhere to be seen but they were pretty sure it wouldn't be long till he reappeared, so they had to make a decision: try to cool the fuel pump down with cold water from the adjacent stream, or risk an enormous bear ripping the door off its hinges and feasting on two tasty humans inside. They'd both seen photos of what black bears can do to cars that had food left inside. And this was a grizzly. And they were the food.

Quickly deducing that the former option was the best call it was then they realized they'd left their thermoses in the packs they'd tossed on the road. What to use? Gabrielle jumped

FOUND

out, opened the hood and noticed the water-squirter bottle, empty of course. Grabbing it tightly she just tore it off its mounting bracket. Carter was duly impressed. He grabbed it from her and ran down the bank, filled it up, stumbled back, and poured it all over the pump and gas line to the carb. Carter ran down refilled as Gabrielle desperately tried to start the Land Rover. Two bottles later it coughed into life! Carter slammed the hood down while hurling himself into the passenger seat as Gabrielle gunned it out of there.

They quickly decided to leave those two samples for another summer, and another crew.

FOUND

5. Edgar's Indecision

"Make up your mind Edgar, we don't have all day."

"Well we actually do have all day but well, OK, what version?"

"Oh here we go again. I thought you'd made up your mind."

"I was so close to ordering the Gullwing but then they go and announce a Roadster version with all sorts of upgrades. But those doors just look so amazing. We live in Oregon so it makes the most sense climate-wise..."

"... and, then you'll say, 'But we'll probably only drive it on nice days anyway so we should get the Roadster,'" Denise interjected.

"Yeah, I know."

"Sir, pardon me, what should I get, I can't for the life of me decide?" Edgar asked the salesman.

"It can get really hot in the coupes, even just on warm days. But with the Roadster you'll lose those amazing doors. But, between you and me, many folks don't like them anyway because it's hard to get in and out.

"The Roadster prices haven't been set as of yet and we don't know when delivery will occur but I've heard they'll be significantly more dear."

"OK, that's it, I'll take the Gullwing in DB 190 Graphite Gray with the blue plaid gabardine interior, Rudge wheels, and the fitted luggage."

"Excellent choice sir. I'll write up an order and get it to New York tout de suite."

"Hello, Mr. Thomas I've got some bad news about your 300SL order. Seems we missed out on ordering it just as they closed the order book and are now only providing Roadsters."

"What?"

"Yes, the Gullwing has been discontinued and they're now only offering the Roadster version."

"You're kidding. I guess my indecision came home to roost."

"And I've called all around and there are no Gullwings unaccounted for."

"OK, I've just got to have one, and only brand new, I've been dreaming of it since the day I saw one at the 1954 New York Auto show. Even spoke with Max Hoffman at length who told me he was the one responsible for getting the executives in Stuttgart to make a production version of the 300SLR."

"Would you like a Roadster in the same color combination then?"

"OK."

FOUND

"Perhaps you're interested in a factory hardtop, best of both worlds?"

"But no Gullwings."

"No sir, sorry."

"How much?"

"We'll cover any additional, sir."

"OK then, but can I have the top in plain silver, I think it's DB 180. That will make for a nice subtle contrast."

"Very well sir. And I apologize once again."

Edgar picked up his gleaming new 300SL Roadster four months later at Portland's Don Rasmussen's Mercedes. The dealer was brand new and had only sold a few cars, but this was their first 300SL delivery so all the employees came out to wave goodbye as Mr. Thomas drove away with Mrs. Thomas trailing far behind in their slow and smelly 190D, Mildred. They were now the only family in town with the top, and bottom, of the Mercedes Benz hierarchy.

On September 3rd, 1959 Edgar came to the door to find a couple of serious suits standing with a court order. Seems Mr. Thomas had been cooking the books for a few years so he could, among other things, finally afford a 300SL. The car, and Mr. Thomas, were both unceremoniously hauled off.

By this time the Roadster had only accumulated 4,287 miles and was exactly like the day it was picked up from Rasmussen's. There weren't many people at the auction, so Conrad thought he just might have a chance at his dream car.

As bidding started however he saw, from the corner of his eye, Mr. Rasmussen himself. Drats. Luckily, bidding took far longer than anticipated and, by the time the 300SL came up, Mr. Rasmussen was nowhere to be seen.

"Do I hear $5,000?"

"Do I hear $4,000?"

"How about $3,000?"

"Come on, as you know this is a 1957 Mercedes Benz

300SL, the fastest car in the world. A new one would set you back around $11 grand. And it's only a couple years old!

"Do I hear $2,500?"

Conrad yelled out, "$1,500."

The auctioneer said, "Do I hear $2,000?" And paddle number 43 went up at the back of the room.

"$2,100?"

And Conrad slowly raised his paddle.

"Do I hear $2,200?"

Conrad held his breath, and heard nothing.

"Going once, going twice, SOLD! to the extremely lucky gentleman wearing a huge grin and black Stetson."

FOUND

6. Plum Crazy

Glenn was a typical Pacific Northwest hard worker. Family man. Married at 19. Kids started appearing at 21 and didn't stop until 30. Friday night poker and beer once a month. Glenn had bought out a local tool rental shop in Snohomish when it was on its last legs; and had turned it into a local chain of seven stores across the western slopes of Washington State.

His 50th birthday was fast approaching and his wife Meredith wanted to do something really special. Something outrageous. Something they'd never typically do. Maybe go backpacking across Europe? Skydive? Buy a big boat? No, she thought: I'll get him his dream car. A '71 'Cuda in Vitamin C with white bucket seats, a 383 and a 4 speed. It would nicely replace his '62 Ford Country Squire wagon with fake wood sides. He really deserved something special; and he'd never pull the trigger himself—too extravagant—too many college funds to fund. Too outrageous.

Perfect.

Glenn's birthday was less than a month away so she knew she'd better get on it. Being the business's accountant she knew she could hide the money from their personal account. Nothing illegal mind you but he certainly didn't need to see a significant payment being made to the Plymouth dealership.

She called a friend's brother Brad who was an atypical slow-talking sales guy at *Cascade Chrysler Plymouth*. She swore him to secrecy. Double-dared him, the whole nine yards.

Did he have such a car?

He laughed and said they were almost always custom ordered; and it would take at least three to four months depending on factory orders.

Giving Glenn an order form in a birthday card would certainly be far less exciting than having a really bright orange 'Cuda rumbling in the driveway when he got home on April 11th.

Brad said he'd call around and see what might be out there on other dealers' lots.

A couple painful days later Brad was on the phone.

"I've got good news and I've got bad news."

"Ok, bad first."

"That specific car doesn't exist anywhere new on anyone's lot both across the States or in Canada."

"Ok, the good?"

"I found a somewhat similar car but it's significantly more expensive. About 50% more. And it's a different color. Plum Crazy."

"This is sounding more like a Kool-Aid commercial. You mean purple?"

"Yup."

"Ok, and...?"

"It's a convertible."

"Brad, you know where we live—it's not sunny Southern

FOUND

California."
"I know, but summers are gorgeous."
"Yeah, all six weeks of them."
"It has a Shaker hood, and an elephant engine."
"Excuse me?"
"An elephant engine - a 426 Hemi. 425 horsepower."
"Well I have no idea what that means but I'm assuming it makes a lot of noise and goes really fast?"
"Yup."
"And eats lots of gas?"
"Yup."
"And Glenn would love it?"
"Yup.
"They're very rare and this car is sitting in a showroom in Kamloops, British Columbia. That's not that far away and we could get the paperwork done so it can be registered here. Supposedly some kid who'd made a lot of money working a ton of overtime in the mill had ordered it but when his parents found out they vetoed it."
"White top and interior?"
"Nope, black top with black interior."
"How much, all-in, sitting in our driveway on the 11th of next month?"
"$4,345.65
"We could get two nice new cars for that much."
"Maybe three."
"Will you take less?"
"Nope."
"Do we get free floor mats?"
"Yup. And a Hurst pistol-grip, Rallye Instrument Cluster, and 3-speed wipers."
"Ok, I'll drop down tomorrow with a check for the down-payment. Would you please call the dealer and tell him it's sold right now though. I can't go through the stress of losing it!"
"Yup."
"Call me back when it's done."
"Yup."
Perfect. Perfectly outrageous.

GREGORY LONG

Fast-forward a couple years and the Hemi had a bunch of old blankets thrown over it in the heated basement garage under the house. He just couldn't bare to look at it, let alone drive it—worst Christmas holiday ever.

7. Refrigerators, Horsemeat, and Tatras

"I went in to buy a refrigerator and almost came out with a Commie car," Scott said to his buddies.

Shorters Electric was, bizarrely, in the business of selling horsemeat, refrigerators, yes, electrical stuff, and had — in the last couple months — taken on a line of Czechoslovakian Tatra automobiles recently launched in Canada. It had an air cooled rear four cylinder engine, similar to that new German car he'd seen recently buzzing about, the Volkswagen.

"They can't give it away. Who wants one of those

communist cars anyway?"

"What do they know about cars?" Scott said as he sprinkled the infield with a Blue for himself, Todd, and Brian.

"Well, as it turns out, a lot. They were a thriving bunch. Prague, before the war, was an amazing place. Architecture, design, and all sorts of intellectual pursuits were commonplace. Tatra had already put into production very fast, stable, and aerodynamic cars back in the mid '30s. And then Hitler rolled in and everything changed overnight. And here in our little town of Victoria sits a brand new Tatra at Shorters Electric. A Tatra Tatraplan T600, to be exact. In shiny black with warm red cloth upholstery."

"I just read in the Colonist that some commie-haters dumped 50 or so just like it off a barge in the Vancouver harbour last week. All brand new and now sitting in Davey Jones locker."

"Idiots," Scott said, "Don't they know they're just trying to rebuild after the destruction of World War II; and are trading cars with Canada for wheat to feed their people?"

"All I know is that someone could make some good coin by scavenging them up off the bottom, drying them out, and selling them."

"You're insane. People won't even buy them if they're sitting here all sparkly, new, and perfectly dry!" Brian exclaimed.

"Good point," Todd said as Brian slugged him in the shoulder. "You've always been the stupid one."

"So sounds like you guys don't think I should buy it, right? I know you idiots are true blue American car guys but the Tatra is just so darn fascinating. Great in the snow and wet with all that weight over the driving wheels, great mileage, lots of room — even a secret hatch behind the back seat to hide your Canadian moonshine," Scott said as they all scanned the brochure with a bright red one on the cover.

"You'll never get parts," Todd said.

"Well, unless you dive to the bottom of Vancouver Harbour," Brian joked.

FOUND

Chris from Shorters called back early the next morning.

"Remember I said "$2,600? How about $2,300? Final offer."

"Against all my good thinking I'll offer you two grand."

"How about $2,200?"

"How 'bout no," Scott said, as he hung up the phone.

"Seems like we got disconnected... how about $2,100?"

Click.

"OK, OK, $2,000. But I need payment tomorrow. Mr. Shorter is on my ass for getting him into this whole Tatra mess in the first place."

"Wait a minute, you're going to stand by it right, 12 month warranty — it says right here in the brochure."

"Well, I was just about to mention that. No warranty. They're not importing them anymore. Seems there was some big problem in Vancouver and that was the last straw. Lots of parts in Montreal though."

Click.

"$1,800 as is. That's it. We're losing our shirt, I'm lucky to have a job."

"OK, I'll bring a cheque tomorrow."

"How about cash?"

"OK, OK, sheesh..."

Table of Cars:

1st Gear: Breakfast
- 1970 BMW 2800 CS Coupe
- 1967 Saab Sonett II

2nd Gear: Lives of Interesting Cars:
1 – 1957 Ferrari 250 Testa Rossa Scaglietti Spyder
2 – 1967 Citroën DS 21 Chapron Décapotable
3 – 1967 Jaguar XK-E Fixed Head Coupe
4 – 1974 Land Rover Series III
5 – 1957 Mercedes Benz 300SL Roadster
6 – 1971 Plymouth Barracuda Convertible
7 – 1950 Tatra Tatraplan T600

3rd Gear: It's a Beautiful Day for a Tatra Hunt

4th Gear: More Lives of Interesting Cars:
8 -
9 -
10 -
11 -
12 -
13 -

5th Gear: Lunch

6th Gear: Even More Lives of Interesting Cars:
14 -
15 -
16 -
17 -
18 -
19 -
20 -

Overdrive: The Garages of Mr. Brant
1 - The Roundhouse
2 - The Crow's Nest
3 - Brantville

3rd Gear:

It's a Beautiful Day for a Tatra Hunt

There were no actual street numbers visible off 136th Avenue, just as Mr. Brant had said, but the gate pillars were even more foreboding than anticipated: They looked straight out of a Scooby-Doo mystery. The one lane gravel road disappeared into the forest but after a few moments Tanner glimpsed a few buildings up high on a hill to the east. As he drew closer he saw what turned out to be a Craftsman masterpiece. The now paved track wended its way around a huge pond, eventually snaking its way up behind the back of the mansion through an amazing English garden.

He turned his Sonett into the picturesque courtyard in front of huge wooden front doors, and parked. He couldn't help but notice an enormous circular building with many garage doors. And was that a large glass crow's nest on the roof?

A few moments later a stunning dark-haired woman with a deep olive complexion in her mid-forties appeared, "You must be Tanner. I'm Keira. My husband said you'd be dropping by for some car-talk."

"Keira's Irish, right?"

"Yes, yes it is."

"So you're Black Irish perhaps?"

"Well aren't we perceptive. Yes, I guess you could say that. Not sure my ancestors were washed up on the shores of Ireland in the late 1500's though," Keira said in her amazing Irish brogue.

"I'll go see what's taking him. Cute car."

Just then Mr. Brant appeared at the door and slowly walked down the steps, holding the bannister firmly.

"You're late. You said 10am."

Glancing at his watch Tanner said, "It's only eight minutes after 10."

"So you are admitting to your rampant tardiness?"

"Yes... but don't I get a grace period."

"Your grace period was seven and a half minutes. And what's with that goofy trailer on the back? I've never seen a Sonett pull a trailer before."

"When one goes on a Tatra hunt one needs to be in a position to bring back some choice booty—like the rear engine hatch with the fin."

"Ah, yes, smart-thinking—like bringing back a seven-point rack. But do you think that trailer can hold more than three pounds?"

"Very funny, I'll have you know I picked up eight bags of mulch with this extremely unassuming robust trailer from Home Depot just last weekend."

"You've just got this car? You drive Savannah and

FOUND

Sutton around in an old Saab sports car?"

"Hutton, her name is Hutton, like Lauren Hutton."

"Oh, I like Lauren Hutton. What were we talking about?"

"My awesome trailer."

"Oh yes, you must have another car too?"

"Yes, we do. We needed a van so I bought a '61 Fiat Multipla."

"Liar. You don't have a Multipla... *do you?*"

"No, you're right, we have a Barkas, and a Powell wagon complete with the sliding fishing pole storage canisters."

"What the Sam Hill!?" Mr. Brant exclaimed.

"OK, not really. We have a Honda Odyssey—Slate Green Metallic that looks blue, with a gray leather interior—it's already been to the moon and is heading back: 242,000 miles and still going strong."

"Great, but still boring, right? I agree vans make the most sense these days; but everyone still wants one of those gargantuan SUV or whatever acronym they refer to them by. How silly. Four-wheel drive, huge tires, and all this other nonsense that's just a waste to drive little Eleanor to school. I use to take all the neighborhood kids in a Mini Countryman. They'd all pile in the back, always struggling to get those little rear wooden-trimmed doors closed. Now every kid has 17 juice-box holders, a couple TVs, and internet access. At least with a van they utilize the space pretty well. Those SUV's just waste space, and fuel. I hate them."

"I see that. Anything else you're as passionate about hating?"

"Punks that drive Saab Sonett III's."

"Whew, missed that by one measly iteration."

"What...? Never mind. Why didn't you take the van to get mulch at Home Depot?"

"Because I like to show-off my trailer, that's why."

"A little touchy on your diminutive utility trailer, huh?"

"Well, my twin brother Devin loves to make fun of my Sonett, my van, my weight, and my diminutive utility trailer. He drives a big-ass pickup truck and has a Harley."

With the banter slowing down they *sort of* jumped into

the Saab just after Mr. Brant yelled, 'shotgun'; and said goodbye to Keira. Keira was ecstatic her husband had met Tanner. He'd been spending more and more time cooped up in the house—and garages—and she was excited he was off on a car adventure. And not just for his sake. Like most woman she just wasn't into old cars. Or new cars for that matter. She was excited to take some time to herself and hang with a few of her best girlfriends. And, well, there was also that guy named Quentin.

"Well, I'm glad we took the Sonett, and the diminutive utility trailer. Let everyone else be comfortable in all their windows-up air-conditioned grandeur, while we zip along in a cramped, loud, harsh, outdated Swedish sports car with a Matchbox trailer. And, Tanner, just so you know, I couldn't be happier."

"Me too Mr. Brant. I'm not sure why we prefer this mode of motoring—not everyday mind you, but as all cars become reliable appliances, our old cars become even more entertaining. Oh yeah, you were talking about Minis. I like original Minis a lot. And the BMW Mini's are nice too. I missed out on an original-owner '65 Mini Cooper S in Farnia Grey years back now—that's one that got away."

"Yup, never owned one before but drove them a lot back in the 60's with friends. The latest Minis are far from mini. They too have jumped on the SUV bandwagon. I guess they're Mini SUVs. I especially like the Mini Moke though. They're in the Mehari, Jolly family. I have a friend who's a Moke fanatic. He left North Seattle about 20, dammit, must be 30 years ago now and moved his four beautiful young girls—and a very accommodating wife—to one of the San Juan Islands up by the Canadian border. Their island had no ferry service so was even more isolated. He searched out—and took over by barge—probably a half dozen Mokes. All in running condition but far from perfect. I believe he said most came from either Hawaii or Catalina Island off the coast of LA.

"Anyway, the girls all ended up going to a one-room school house, one of the last standing in the US. Each morning they'd jump in a Moke, drive the dirt track to their vessel, boat 20 minutes along a tiny inlet, moor, pick up another Moke on

FOUND

the other side, and drive the final five miles to school. They did this everyday, no matter the weather. I frankly can't think of many worse vehicles to do this in especially because of the rain. The Moke has a very poor fabric roof. But they're in the rain-shadow so I guess that helped a little bit. Crazy though.

"He said he'd use one until it had some malady, then grab another and — every seven to ten years — he'd barge one or two over to the mainland and drive or tow them to Bellingham where a guy would fix up the bodies and drivetrains, and off they'd go again. Girls have all grown up and moved away but he still keeps a drove of them. Wonderful guy. Boy, I wish I could remember his name."

"A drove?"

"Yes, drove. A group of donkeys is a drove and a Moke is a donkey. Come on man do I need to spell everything out to you?"

"Clearly you do but I can also imagine you're full of crap."

"Look it up in your Funk and Wagnalls."

"Funk and who?"

"Funk and Wagnalls. You're worse off than I thought."

"You want me to look up a made-up word in the a made-up dictionary?"

"Conrad! Conrad Cullen!"

"What?"

"The guy's name with the Mokes. Conrad Cullen."

"Can I change topics now?"

"By all means. As long as it's about cars. Old cars."

"It is. I also have an interesting French two-door that was a contemporary of the Sonett. Care to guess?"

"French, two-door, mid-sixties? Well, let's see, Simca 1000 Coupe?"

"Nope, but I like your style. Weirder. And more interesting."

"4 cylinder?"

"Nope."

"6?"

"Nope."

"Ahhh, a Panhard 24 BT, right?"

"God you're good. Wow."

"You've got one, around here?" Mr. Brant asked somewhat shocked.

"Yup, but it's in bits right now. Waiting for a clutch and rear brake light activator from France."

"Well I must see it. You can see how the DS's then new front-end in '68 clearly borrowed from the 24. But that was OK as Citroën had swallowed them up by then."

"Agreed. But the Panhard's didn't swivel around corners."

"Good point, but the Tatra, Tucker, and Ruxton had a similar feature decades before even Citroën."

"There's some controversy around that, Mr. Brant. Have you ever seen one of those models where the headlights were actually steered by the steering wheel?"

"Well, no, but I'm going to dig into my books to confirm. And why is there what looks to be a bite mark in the armrest here?"

"Well, that's an interesting story: one day I'm taking Savannah out for a drive and I've got her all strapped in her car seat and I notice she's being really quiet and looks to be staring close up at the door panel. I asked her what's going on and she quickly turns around and says, nuthin'. Obviously something was up so I looked a little deeper and, sure enough, she'd been gnawing on the armrest! Boy, was I mad—at the time. Now I rather like it. Funny how such disastrous events in time diminish into 'whatever's'."

"Yup, that armrest can never be replaced."

"I need gas. Let's get off at this exit," Tanner said.

As they pulled up to the pumps a couple of guys appeared and asked the usual two questions: *'What is it? And what year is it?'*

"A Saab. A 1967 Saab," Mr. Brant replied with just a murmur of disdain.

"A Saab. Don't look like any Saab I've ever seen. Pretty impressive trailer though," the older man in a *Caterpillar* trucker hat said with a laugh.

"It's pretty cool if you ask me," said the other who might have been his son. "It ain't no '74 Satellite Sebring Sundance, mind you, but it's pretty sweet nonetheless."

FOUND

With that, Tanner jumped back in the Sonett and off they went.

"I take you for a microcar enthusiast Tanner. Especially given your proven proclivity for diminutive utility trailers. Do you have any of those?"

"No, not yet; but my old girlfriend's grandmother had the coolest little car hidden in her basement and it was a microcar. Her grandfather had won it in a sweepstakes from Playboy Magazine.

"He was really happy.

"And boy was his wife mad.

"So mad in fact she removed the sliding glass door into the basement and drove the Goggomobil right in. Then put the door back on, threw a blanket over it, and hid the key. Sadly her husband was killed at work the following week and they hadn't made up. What's the old adage, 'Never go to bed angry?'"

"If that was the case I'd never have slept my entire first, and second, marriages," Mr. Brant quickly retorted.

"So how'd you find car?"

"I was playing ping-pong in the basement with Cath one afternoon and, while looking around for the ball, I couldn't believe what I'd come across. Cath said they weren't allowed to talk about it because it made Grannie really sad. Hmmm, I haven't thought about that Gogo for years. I wonder if it's still there?"

"You should check. If you're a true barnfinder you wouldn't be able to sleep until you tracked it down. Did your dad drive interesting cars?"

"Nope, my mom was car crazy, not my dad. Dad one year had bought a fairly new 4-door hardtop Buick Wildcat with every conceivable option but AC. Blue Mist, with black vinyl roof and interior. Just the car for the lower mainland of British Columbia, but not for the Fraser Canyon, during the height of summer, at 2pm when it was something like 106 degrees as we drove to our family cabin. Loaded up with four kids, a Cocker Spaniel with three legs, and a cat that couldn't be trusted. The cat and dog didn't get along at the best of times but after eight hours in a stifling hot car wrapped in wet towels, not so much. And a mum and dad who also, right then, didn't get along much either.

"'I can't believe you didn't get air conditioning. I thought we'd agreed it was essential. Don't you wish you'd have listened to me now?' my mum fumed.

"'I know but it's only a few days each year so we can just grin and bear it,' Dad shot back.

"Just then a blast of steam started pouring out from under the hood and front grill. We pulled over when we found a safe spot where we wouldn't plummet to our death into the rushing waters below. Dad wasn't much of a mechanic so we just all stared at each other until my brother Devin popped open the hood and saw one of the radiator hoses had just come off, spilling its contents all over the road.

"Mum and my little brother took Arfie and Pixie down to a flat spot with tumbleweeds beside the highway and noticed a fruit stand about a mile north. Bob stayed with mum and Monty; and Devin, dad and I ventured off to the mirage. It was only a couple minutes before a pickup pulled over. Dad hopped in the front and Devin and I jumped in the truck's bed.

"We walked up to the fruit stand but it was closed. We heard a commotion coming from down the hill by a little house on the riverside. Dad decided we'd come this far so we ventured down the steep, dirt track to the house.

"A portly, smiling gentleman appeared as we walked towards the front door. No shotgun. A good sign. He told us in a thick Italian accent he'd actually run out of fruit and was going to pick some more in the evening when it had cooled down a bit. He'd also been expecting a load of corn from Chase. He then noticed me hearing splashing and children's voices and said, 'Want to go for a quick dip?'

"Would I!" I quickly responded. Devin concurred.

"'But I guess you're just going to have to go in your underwear, if your dad's OK with that, I mean. Sophia and Annette would love to have a couple of strapping young men as guests I bet.'

"As I peeked around the corner there was an above ground pool, not too big but full of water, cool water, sourced directly from the fast running river below. And two beautiful teenagers. As we rounded the corner in our underwear they let out blood curdling screams as we cannonballed right off their

FOUND

wobbly deck into the sparkling oasis.

"Over the ensuing years we always stopped at Lorenzo's on the way up, and back. Giant bags of cherries were my favourite; and mum would always say, 'Don't eat too many, you'll get the trots.'

"Our family became great summer friends with the Andretti's — he said 'no relation' before I even asked — and they'd come stay at our log cabin for a few days each August even though it was their busiest time of the year. That was always my favourite part of summer vacation especially playing Wide World, swimming out to the Taylor's wharf, collecting frogs when we were younger; and other stuff with Annette as we got older. We all eventually went off to University and our own ways."

"Tell me more about the 'other stuff with Annette," Mr. Brant inquired.

"Dirty old man," Tanner replied as Mr. Brant just laughed.

"Lorenzo eventually ended up buying the old Wildcat for a song from my dad. There was a weird knock in the engine and a shimmy in the suspension. Lorenzo drove it for years afterwards, even without air conditioning. I'd love it when he'd bring it back to the lake each summer, mostly because of Annette but also to see the old Buick.

"Their once colourful fruit stand became a dilapidated shack as traffic dwindled on the Cariboo Highway partially because of the new Coquihalla to Kamloops. Lorenzo eventually sold the land and headed back to the old country; and we lost track of the girls. Who would have thought that a horrendously unpleasant experience could have turned into my first true love? Silver lining, or what?"

"The Cariboo Highway and the Fraser River bring back fond memories for me too, Tanner. We use to do that route each summer for years to stay up at Green Lake, just in from 70 Mile House."

"That's where our place is Mr. Brant! Where'd you stay?"

"My second ex wife's family had a little cabin there I just loved. It was odd — I met her on the beach in California and she ended up being from Vancouver Island and had a cabin in the Cariboo. The cabin was made of fence posts. They were assembled vertically to create walls. As an architect I found it rather ingenious: simple, beautiful, cheap, and easy to build. And it was right on the lake. No electricity or running water. My wife wasn't nearly as fond of it but Carter and I loved it. Never any fish in the lake though.

"Do you know about the old bridge that goes across the Fraser River, just down from Hell's Gate?" Mr. Brant questioned.

"Sure do, Alexandra Bridge. We'd always look for it from the new Alexandra Bridge—you can just see it for a few seconds as you zoom by, looking north. We'd often stop, hike down over the railway tracks, and walk across the bridge. As you know it's pretty disconcerting as the bridge's road surface is made up of metal bars spaced a few inches apart so it's like walking on air above white water rapids."

"OK, but do you know about the secret tunnel near Hell's Gate?"

"Nope, where?"

"If I tell you it won't be secret," Mr. Brant replied.

"If you don't tell me I'll hold my breath until I turn blue. I've got lots of practice holding my breath in those seven tunnels in the canyon."

"I'm waiting," Mr. Brant said coolly.

"Uncle, you win," Tanner said quickly as he exhausted his lungs.

"I use to travel that highway when it was one lane dirt in parts. This is going way back now. We used to drive across the original Alexandra Bridge when we'd go up to Babine, Lakelse, Ootsa Lake, and Rupert over to the Queen Charlottes to fish for a month. Oh yeah, and a tiny settlement called Osland where Icelandic settlers in the late 1800's came to homestead on the salmon-rich Skeena River. The town was connected by boardwalks instead of sidewalks. I wonder if any of it still exists? Anyway, those were amazing trips. Once I remember fishing with an old guy that drove a suicide door Lincoln convertible, '62 I think. It was fascinating to see it all the way up there close to Alaska but even more fascinating was the license plate: It had 4 stars on it. He was a real 4 star General, then

FOUND

retired.

"Anyway, as you're travelling north on the Trans-Canada there's a restaurant that, until fairly recently, had a giant Elvis sign out front on the left and, just after it is the Hell's Gate tunnel. If you park near Elvis's place..."

"Graceland, you mean?" Tanner chimed in.

"Not funny... and walk towards the tunnel but veer off to your left and hike up a bit you'll find the secret tunnel. It was the original one I use to drive through. It's just a giant blasted tunnel with no concrete liner so over the years thousands of rocks have fallen and littered the floor. Trying to make it through without a rock hitting you in the head is rather fun."

"You call that fun?"

"Tough guys find it fun, Tanner."

"OK, I've got one more for you," Tanner said excitedly.

"Do you know the ladders near Hell's Gate?"

"Fish ladders, yes."

"No, wooden people ladders. As you're heading north on the last major curve before you get to the Hell's Gate tramway look up. *Way up.* You'll see the remnants of a set of wooden stairs, more like ladders actually, that lie against almost sheer cliffs. I assume some brave soul with the Highways Department had to scale the rickety old ladder to dislodge rocks from above: sort of like avalanche control but for boulders. When I was a kid the whole set was there, now only a couple spans remain. Check it out before they're all gone. I think the Canadian photographer Edward Burtynsky has a photo of the ladders hanging in the National Gallery of Art in Ottawa, or perhaps it's the McMichael Collection on the outskirts of Toronto? Can't remember."

"I will certainly do that but I don't get up there very often any more."

"How 'bout we do a road trip up to the cabin. We still have it. Doesn't get much use anymore."

"I would so *love* to do that—we can try to do as many of these special Fraser Canyon side-trips as my ol' legs will carry me. And talking about rock slides reminds me of a story I use to tell Carter when he was little—I bet your girls would like it."

"OK, I'm game."

"I'm sure you've seen those signs that say "Watch For

Falling Rock"; well, now they all seem to have a little image of rocks falling, but do you know what they mean?"

"Um, yes, Mr. Brant. They advise drivers to be aware that rocks may fall down from the cliffs above."

"Nope. Common misconception."

"Once upon a time… there was as an Indian, I mean First Nations, tribe that lived in the canyon. Their leader, Chief Skookumchuck, was having a potlatch to celebrate the coming salmon spawn and had everyone out foraging for delicacies of the forest. His youngest son was dying to participate but claimed he was ready to go off by himself, no longer needing to be chaperoned by his older siblings. Chief nervously agreed and told the boy to go only down as far as the small stream that flowed into the mighty Fraser. Everyone went off and collected berries, greens, roots and edible bark. One of the young males bagged a beautiful Bighorn.

"The young boy was enjoying his freedom. He splashed in the cold stream looking for frogs. Then, spying a golden fox with a wispy white tail, he followed her over hill and dale. How amazing it would be if he'd brought one back for his father. It was easy for the creature to lose the young boy who had by then found himself in uncharted territory. His father had always told him to just sit down and stay put if he ever got lost. So he did.

"A short time later Chief noticed his young son wasn't back and walked down to the stream expecting to see the boy wading in the water. But nothing. He walked quickly down to the Fraser and saw no trace of anyone being there recently.

"He ran back to his village and called the tribe to assemble. He broke them into search party groups and off they went in every direction. They searched till dark and reassembled at first light. This went on for a fortnight until Chief called it off."

"Hey wait Mr. Brant, there's one of those signs now!" Tanner interrupted.

"Well that was nicely scripted… so when the white men came through first mining for gold, then building the railroad, Chief told them about his lost little son. And when the highway first bore its way through the almost impenetrable forest, he told them too. And that's when they first erected the 'Watch for Falling Rock' signs that live on today. And 'Falling Rock', to the

FOUND

best of my knowledge, has never been found."

"I had no idea Mr. Brant, excellent. Hutton, especially, will love that; and I'll never look at those signs the same way again.

"But do you know what little Falling Rock should have done?" Tanner asked. "He should have taken a pack of playing cards — ignore the fact they wouldn't have any back then, as it ruins my feeble attempt at my one joke — sat down and played solitaire because, sure as heck, someone would come along and tell him to put the 9 on the 10."

"That's actually pretty funny. Do you play crib?"

"Love crib. I could easily skunk you. Yes, Mr. Brant, I'm that good," Tanner joked.

"Bit cocky I see. Good, it'll be more embarrassing when I whoop ya," Mr. Brant stated.

"You ever get a 29?"

"Yes. Only once," Mr. Brant replied. "At a bar on Salt Spring Island in the late 70's. I bought the whole place a round. And, of course, it was summer and packed solid. I then told them they should be the ones buying me drinks — now that wasn't smart. I returned a few years ago on my friend Brad's boat and, sure enough, they'd put the actual 29 hand's cards up in a frame on the wall with my name on a little plaque."

"Awesome. And maybe we shouldn't play for money after all..." Tanner said sheepishly.

"Oh, and by the way I've even got another sign story. Not many people have one sign story, but I have two."

"Lucky you Mr. Brant."

"No lucky you, Mr. Hamilton. But first, do you know what the Lazy 3 is?"

"This, I assume, is a joke?"

"No, it's related to the railways," Mr. Brant said as he pulled out a hankie and blew his nose extremely loudly.

"Wow, how do you do that?"

"What?"

"Blow your nose with the sound of a locomotive?"

"Practice."

"Don't you wake the children? I've never seen anyone under the age of 80 use a hankie, by the way. They're pretty gross... *aren't they?*"

"Your generation is suppose to be all about recycle, reuse, re-something..."

"Reduce," Tanner quickly responded. "I guess you're right. Never thought of it that way. Still seems pretty gross though. I sure wouldn't want to be a hankie manufacturer. Or a flashlight factory for that matter."

"Why?"

"Because they're in every phone now."

"Ah, yes, just like cameras, and slide-rules."

"Slide-rules?"

"Yes, manual calculators."

"What?"

"Now, back to the Lazy 3?"

"I still have no idea what you're talking about."

"Next time you're in the Canyon, look for a Canadian National railway car — the CN, and see if you can see a Lazy 3."

"Or just look it up on my iPhone?"

"No, you must see it live. Stupid phones," Mr. Brant grumbled. "Amazing devices actually and I wouldn't go anywhere in my old cars without one but it takes some of the fun out of life when you can just Google anything, at anytime, doesn't it? Or is that just the old coot in me rearing its head again?"

"I do find them more good than bad Mr. Brant. The worst part of all is how we've all turned into zombies — me included — just staring into these little screens all the time. People my age and up still have a modicum of respect to put it down when speaking with someone but the younger generation, I'm afraid, is growing up with them 'natively' and it'll become more and more commonplace to have their noses in them 24-7."

"So, back to my second sign story if you don't mind Mr. Hamilton: My wife was at a BC government function with me when we were first developing Whistler and we were talking to the BC Minister of Highways. There had to be a lot of investment in the highway infrastructure to get Whistler really off the ground so we were lobbying him. And by lobbying, back then, and in BC, meant that someone had told me the Minister drove a DS which I thought amazing given you'd think he'd have serious ties to the US/Canada motor industry. I sauntered over and told him I too drove a Citroën. He asked which model and I told him a DS and 2CV—this was before the SM was imported. We were friends immediately. I asked him why he drove a Citroën especially because his riding was way up in Rupert but he said that when Detroit, or Windsor, built a car as safe as the DS he'd drive one of theirs.

"My wife then offered a rather amazing, insightful, observation to us both. She said, 'We have lot of accidents when people try to pass and don't have either the road they need, or the line of sight, or both, right?'

"'Yes, people are always taking chances at the edges and it costs hundreds of deaths per year', Mr. Lea said.

"'Well, why don't you just put up signs a couple miles before passing lanes appear? That way people won't take as much risk as they'll know they have an extra lane in just a mile or two?' my wife wondered.

"'I pay a lot of people, a lot of money, to enhance highway safety and that's the best, most common sense approach I've ever heard. Excuse me, you've got me completely intrigued and, if I can find a phone around here, I'm going to call my Deputy Minister and see if there's any history on such an idea.' Mr. Lea said excitedly.

"A few minutes later the Minister reappeared, 'Mrs. Brant', he said. 'In all his years he'd never seen or heard of it'; and that the concept was brilliant. He was going to immediately test it out on some of the worst stretches in the province.

"I saw him at a function a few years later and he came right up to report that the signs had significantly reduced fatalities on highways across the province. He asked where my wife was and I had to tell him we'd divorced but—as she was the mother of my son—we still stay in touch and I'd let her know. I then asked him how his DS was and he said it had finally gotten so rusty it wasn't safe and—as he couldn't buy a new one because of the new safety standards, which he thought rather ironic—he bought a Saab."

"So… back to your family: You said your mom was car

crazy. How crazy?"

"Certifiable.

"She was a psychology professor at the local university; and, actually, I'm kind of a famous guy. If you google Tanner Hamilton you'll get a ton of hits. My mum had this hypothesis in the 70's that somehow all the people we meet in our life have a profound effect on our future. We just don't know how. So, from the day, I mean moment, I was born she kept a list of everyone, and I mean everyone, who came in contact with me. Starting with the doctor, the nurses, the hospital staff, the milkman, the cashier at the grocery store, the gas station attendant, everybody. She would, if she could, mark down their name, approximate height, weight, skin colour, gender of course, and if they seemed to have a happy, neutral, or unhappy disposition.

"It became even more bizarre when I started school and had to report back with the data nightly. Yearbooks became extremely valuable as we could go through them easily and evaluate every child. I finally told her I couldn't do this any longer when I went off to college."

"You did this until you were around 18?!"

"Yes sir, and she's still working on the paper. And I have no idea the outcome. But, in certain anorak circles, I'm as popular as Brad Pitt."

"Well, she couldn't have driven something as pedestrian as a Datsun or Pontiac, then. What did she drive? Where did you get your appreciation for collector cars? It certainly wasn't from your dad's Buick."

"Definitely my mum, as you'll see. Mum was the kiss of death to an import car company. If she bought your car, you were doomed. And she bought a lot of new cars. It made no sense. Dad just merrily went on his way with Buicks, and the odd pickup truck—not that he needed to pickup anything, he just liked them. Especially ones with huge engines, for which he had no use since he never trailered or hauled anything: He just liked to be prepared in case that day ever came.

"But Mum's car history is truly amazing—so phenomenal in fact I've committed it to memory. At 16 her dad bought her a new Skoda Felicia convertible in Caribbean Blue with Saddle interior. That was in 1960. Next up was a Lagoon

FOUND

Blue '63 Amphicar 770 — 7 knots and 70 mph — but it only lasted until her drunk friend Chappy forgot to latch the extra door lock and opened it in the middle of Elk Lake. It was replaced by a '65 DKW F11 in Jade Green over Shell White, but traded for a Eucalyptus Green with Vellum Print upholstery '67 Humber Super Snipe IV in 1969. I have no idea why she wanted that car at 25 but she loved it.

"In 1972 she bought a brand new Citroën D Special in Bleu Camargue with a Noir Targa interior. On the way home from the factory dealership on Burrard Street in Vancouver she tried her fancy new AM/FM radio just as the CBC announced Citroën was curtailing importation of the DS. Sadly it was T-boned and written off just a few years later. She then bought a 1975 Austin America in Burnt Braken Orange from *Plimley's*. It boggles the mind to think what that transition was like. The Austin lasted just a year as mum had her eye on the Bricklin SV-1. This was 1976 and I was seven. That was clearly an awesome time in my life, to say the least. It was in Safety Orange with a Phoenix Brown interior. Incidentally, one of my favourite car colour names of all time is Bricklin's Safety Suntan, a sort of flesh colour — and you wonder why they didn't last. Mum loved that they were built in Canada: 'We're driving a real Canadian car from New Brunswick', she'd say, even as the doors kept malfunctioning. She certainly did love that thing.

"In 1980 she bought a new Rover 3500. I kid you not. Avocado with Nutmeg leather. It was, obviously, the worst car she ever owned. Such a beautiful innovative design but you couldn't get it down the driveway without something going wrong, or falling off. That lasted only two years and I can't imagine what we lost in depreciation on that baby.

"Then an '82 DeLorean DMC 12. She was taken with the stainless steel body and, of course, the doors. But it didn't have enough room so she traded it for an '85 Merkur XR4Ti in Strato Silver Metallic with Spice Brown leather. Are you finding this comical, Mr. Brant?"

"Beyond comical, this is truly amazing. Your memorization of car colors is also truly scary. I'm assuming there was a Sterling in her future?"

"Yup!"

"No way, I was joking!"

GREGORY LONG

"Yes, a 1990 Sterling 827SLi, in Flame Red. But it came after her first foray into Eastern Bloc cars. Remember, Canada got some wonderful oddities the US didn't. She gave me the Merkur, which was pretty cool as a 16 year old; and she got a '86 Dacia 1410 GTL in Beige—that was the actual colour's name in the marketing material— and then a '89 Skoda 135GLi in China Blau—yes, blau— that got crunched only a year old so that's when she moved to the Sterling. She was all over the place, one year a luxurious car, the next a Czechoslovakian run-about.

"But in 1990 she also bought a Citroën 2CV. It was from a couple of brothers importing them from France as new-old cars. It was aptly called *Escargot Motorcars*. They'd buy an old rust-free frame in Southern France and replace everything on it with new components. New engines, body panels, everything but the frame was changed out; and the frame was painted bright green or blue to show it had all been apart. She saw it at a pretty swanky booth, considering, at the *Toronto International AutoShow* when she was out there for some conference. She ordered a Rouge Delage AC 446, and Noir Onyx AC 200 Charleston and actually still has it. I've enjoyed that car for years too."

"I have that exact car in my other garage but have always boringly called it a Burgundy and Black Charleston," Mr. Brant said sarcastically. "It's also an Escargot car. Does she still have her picnic basket and champagne bottle? I'm really liking your mom, by the way."

"Yes, and I remember one of Escargot's tongue-in-cheek marketing slogans—they'd had only one warranty claim: a plate in one of the car's picnic basket broke. Mum still has her basket, and the little plaque on the dash too.

"Care to guess what came next? It was in 1992 and is arguably the funniest one yet. She bought it in April, five days before they announced they were done."

"Yugo."

"Correcto. In—I kid you not—'Snow White.'"

"Simply amazing," Mr. Brant exclaimed.

"And we're not over yet. I loved that she was buying all this weird stuff but I was also advising her to buy a Toyota Camry, or something Japanese. But she loved buying weird cars. Everyone hates buying cars period, but she loved it; she'd go out of her way to find the most ridiculous pseudo-dealer who was just barely eking out a living."

"So, then what?"

"The Yugo did quite well, surprisingly, and was replaced by a Lada Samara in Snowdrift in '98. Lada had actually sold a lot of cars in Canada. I remember reading they had up to 70 dealers at one time; but it started to crumble when the Koreans entered the market with the Hyundai Pony which, not surprisingly, she didn't buy.

"And then, in 2001 she bought a Saab 9-3 Viggen in Laser Red with a Rocky Black interior — I can't make that up — and she's never looked back. She's put a ton of mileage on it and while it's had issues over that time I can't drag it from her little age-spotted hands. She uses the 2CV on nice days and the Saab on all others.

"Now you surely understand, in excruciating detail, where this weird car collecting gene came from."

"I certainly do. You've clearly come across it honestly."

"So, where'd you get the *Hudson's Bay* point blanket?" Mr. Brant said as he spied it on the rear shelf of the Sonett.

"My parents wedding present years ago," Tanner answered.

"You know old ones are worth good money now, right? How many beaver pelts is it worth?"

"Another common misconception, Mr. Brant."

"Bullcrap. The number of thin black lines signify how many beaver pelts the native Indians traded for a blanket back in the 1700 and 1800's. The bigger the blanket, the more lines, the more pelts."

"Like I said, common misconception. Thought the same thing for years but it's an urban legend. Or a rural legend, actually, I guess, get it?"

"Nope. And I still call bullcrap."

"Look it up. You have the technology."

Mr. Brant grabbed his phone, adjusted his glasses, strained his eyes and read from Wikipedia:

"In the North American fur trade, point blankets were one of the main European items sought by native peoples in exchange for

beaver pelts..."

"See, see, told you so!"
"Keep reading please," Tanner said calmly.
"Lost my place, OK, I'll start again. No interrupting."
"You're the one that interrupted your own reading," Tanner said in mock astonishment.
"I said stop interrupting," Mr. Brant scolded.

"In the North American fur trade, point blankets were one of the main European items sought by native peoples in exchange for beaver pelts, buffalo robes, pemmican, moccasins, and other trade goods. They were desired because of wool's ability to hold heat even when wet, and because they were easier to sew than bison or deer skins.

"Wool cloth of one kind or another was traded as far back as the French regime in North America (1534-1765), but HBC point blankets were introduced in 1780 to compete with similar blankets offered by the Montreal-based private traders. The blankets were often produced with a green stripe, red stripe, yellow stripe and indigo stripe on a white background; the four stripe colours were popular and easily produced using good colourfast dyes at that time.

"OK here we are, Value System:

"In the point system, the points — thin indigo lines — are woven into the blanket to denote its size and weight, such that it need not be unfolded and measured for those facts to be known. A common misconception is that each point indicated a quantity of..."

"Yes? Mr. Brant, you seem to have trailed off at the words common misconception."
"I must have lost my place. No, my battery died. Perhaps, I got a phone call. Damn it. OK, OK...

"A common misconception is that each point indicated a quantity of beaver pelts or Hudson's Bay Company money. Blankets varied in colour, weight and design.

"Still don't believe it. Anyone can put anything up there on Wikipedia. I'm calling The Bay and asking them."

FOUND

"Knock yourself out, Mr. Brant: 'Old Guy on line 9, Old Guy on line 9.'"

"Your map says to get off at the next exit."

"Where are your manners, Mr. Brant?"

"Sorry... please get the hell off at the next exit or I'll make even more fun of your diminutive utility trailer, and your dumb blanket."

"That's better," Tanner said.

"I should have brought a machete," Tanner mentioned as he surveyed the gnarly bush.

Tanner told Mr. Brant to sit back and he'd do the 'pruning' but Mr. Brant would have nothing to do with that.

"I've come down here for a Tatra hunt and I'm gonna hunt."

After about a half hour they'd made a tunnel into the blackberry patch and reached the Tatra. Being August the blackberries were ripe. And delicious. So sweet in fact that it had significantly increased the time it took for them to reach the Tatra.

When they finally got to it, it was clear there wasn't much left. Its once red paint was almost all gone, the interior was a rat's nest, and the cool rear trunk lid, with its dorsal fin, was already missing. And rust was everywhere. It was never going to be exhumed, ever.

"Well that was a bloody well good waste of time. I really wanted to get that engine lid with those cool split windows and dorsal fin," Tanner said, dejectedly.

It was then Mr. Brant saw a glint of sunshine from about 30 feet deeper into the thicket. Was that another car in there? More pruning and Tanner confirmed it wasn't just another car but another Tatraplan.

Cutting a swath around the rear of Tatra Number 1 and, after another hour of hell, millions of thorns, bugs, and beads of sweat, Tanner finally made it to the other beast. This one was black with plenty of reddy primer showing through. There was still an old license plate surround attached that shouted, Shorters Electric, Victoria BC, but no license plate.

This one was in far better shape. Seemed no one had ever screwed around with it. All the windows were intact, the interior, while wet and incredibly moldy was all there. Gauges still in the dash. Steering wheel even steered.

Upon opening the glove compartment-cum-fusebox, they saw some very old, very moist papers. Taking them out of their resting place they brought them out into the light and could just make out '1950 Tatra T600' but everything else was gone except for the registration date of 1971.

They carved their way to the hood and found the spare wheel, the jack, and a huge mouse nest made from the interior's stuffing. The serial number plate was gone too. Weird, they thought.

"Hey, I think there's a compartment behind the rear seats. Who knows what we'll find there," Mr. Brant said.

Tanner struggled to get the rear door open and when he finally got in he unclasped the two rusted latches on the rear interior window and flipped it forward towards the roof and set the stop. It was clear no one had been back there for eons as there was an old knapsack, wrapped in what looked like a perished parachute.

Tanner clumsily hoisted it from the rear compartment and dragged them both out of the brambles and into the sunlight.

"Well that's certainly a parachute—what's left of it anyway. And there's probably a bunch of tools in that bag, or human bones," Mr. Brant said with a hint of foreboding in his voice.

But there were neither.

The bills were stacked in neat piles. US $20's, lots of them. A quick count of a stack, some fast math, and Tanner said, "Wow, I make it close to $200,000."

Mr. Brant sat slowly back on the warm grass and hypothesized, "Do you know who is the longest running FBI hijacking fugitive in US history—who's never been found?"

"DB somebody? He jumped out the back of a passenger plane in the early seventies around here with a knapsack full of cash. And, thankfully, a parachute."

"DB Cooper, but that wasn't his real name. Obviously this is his loot and 'chute. Loot and 'chute, I like that… you should call the police."

"Why me?" Tanner asked with a strain in this voice.

"Because you're so photogenic: Your picture is going to be on every newspaper around the world."

"Hey we're in this together, Mr. Brant. When we're invited to the White House you're coming too."

"I don't like the limelight: Hate it, in fact. Why don't you just take the money? You keep it all, and buy yourself a slightly more manly trailer, fund both your daughters' college funds, get a 60's Mini Cooper S, a Moke, and a Barkas van to boot."

Table of Cars:

1st Gear: Breakfast
- 1970 BMW 2800 CS Coupe
- 1967 Saab Sonett II

2nd Gear: Lives of Interesting Cars:
1 – 1957 Ferrari 250 Testa Rossa Scaglietti Spyder
2 – 1967 Citroën DS 21 Chapron Décapotable
3 – 1967 Jaguar XK-E Fixed Head Coupe
4 – 1974 Land Rover Series III
5 – 1957 Mercedes Benz 300SL Roadster
6 – 1971 Plymouth Barracuda Convertible
7 – 1950 Tatra Tatraplan T600

3rd Gear: It's a Beautiful Day for a Tatra Hunt
- 1967 BMC Mini Moke
- 1967 Panhard 24BT
- 1968 Buick Wildcat
- 1972 Citroën 2CV
- 2001 Saab 9-3 Viggen

4th Gear: More Lives of Interesting Cars:
8 -
9 -
10 -
11 -
12 -
13 -

5th Gear: Lunch

6th Gear: Even More Lives of Interesting Cars:
14 -
15 -
16 -
17 -
18 -
19 -
20 -

FOUND

Overdrive: The Garages of Mr. Brant
   1 - The Roundhouse
   2 - The Crow's Nest
   3 - Brantville

FOUND

4th Gear:

More Lives of Interesting Cars

GREGORY LONG

8. Attempted Murder

"Really? Crush 'em all?"

"Yup, that's the order from headquarters see," as Arnaud showed the other driver Jacque the work order.

"How could that happen? They were just on the floor of the Palais delighting potential buyers last week, and now they're to be destroyed?"

"Qui, seems like murder, doesn't it?"

"What happened?"

"I heard through the grapevine they don't have the means to build out and sell so many different versions. They're going to stick with the smaller engine cars as they'll sell in higher numbers and hopefully bring financial stability back to Citroën. And also something about the axles breaking from too much horsepower."

"Mr. Citroën must be devastated. If you believe what you read in the paper he's not well — it certainly must have been exhausting to drive the creation of the Traction. I can't wait to try one. I'd obviously love to drive the V8 version but alas, that's not to be."

"Are you sure?"

"What do you mean?"

"Maybe we just try one before we drop them off at the crushers?"

"Are you crazy? We'd be fired immediately."

"Who cares? This is a crappy job anyway. Don't you think we could find another right away? Let's get all six loaded and talk about it as we head over there."

The 1934 Paris Auto Salon at the Grand Palais was Citroën's showcase for its radically innovative new Traction Avant. Shown in four, six, and eight cylinders; and in two-door coupe, convertible, and four door sedan versions, it was Andre Citroën's crowning glory after founding the company in 1919. Citroën's first truly brand new car ever, the Traction was named after its Front Wheel Drive technology. It was the first time such an advanced feature was available in a production car. Add to that rack and pinion steering; a monocoque body shell that could withstand rollover crashes while handling like on rails — and you had a milestone in automotive history.

The Traction's introduction came at a time of heavy losses in terms of health, both from the company's coffers, and Andre's. They'd spent heavily on the development of the Traction but still weren't happy with a four speed gearbox and constant velocity joints they'd tried to perfect, so they went back to using a three-speed box.

"I can do this myself Jacque," Arnaud said after they'd winched them all on the transporter. "In fact I've got a little stop-over I'd like to make anyway."

"What kind of stop-over?"

FOUND

"The best kind."

"Ahhh, you ass. You give Frenchman such a bad name."

"Where should I drop you? I won't say anything, if you don't. You'll still get your hours."

"*Le Pt't Bar*, of course. Nothing like a few Belgian beer at ten in the morning."

After dropping Jacque off, Arnaud headed southwest towards Trappes, to a farm that had been in his family for generations.

"Arnaud, what are you doing here? Especially with a truck full of new cars."

"Not just new cars Grandpa, they're the new 22CV Citroëns."

"Didn't I just read about those in the paper?"

"Probably. I'm taking them to the crusher to be destroyed."

"What?" Grand-père said in astonishment.

"Seems like they're not going into production after all so they're destroying them. I have no idea why, but I have the signed work order to take the six of them and drop them off for execution."

"Well now this is making a bit more sense. So you're stealing them, Arnaud?"

"I never thought of it that way gramps: I'm saving them. And not all of them. Just one."

"Which one?"

"Which one do you think?"

"Obviously the one on the bottom, on the back. And it's the convertible, of course. That's the one I'd take if given the chance, too."

"Well you do sort of have a chance Grand-papa. Can I put her in your barn? Way at the back, under these heavy tarps I brought? And then we cover her with hay."

"Arnaud, I don't think so, it's stealing. I can't condone that. What would Jolette say, she'd have my hide."

"Why does she have to know? Is she home?"

"No."

"Come on pépère I know this is crazy but if that beauty gets crushed into a little block of metal, it'll be gone forever. Isn't it bad enough all the others will be eradicated? We have to do our duty to France and save this magnificent French artwork. It's like allowing a Matisse, a Derain, a Sisley or Monet to be thrown into a blazing hearth. Come on pépère, do it for France."

"What are you going to do with it?"

"I have no idea other than they're going to wonder where the hell I am if I don't get over there soon. I don't know what I'm going to tell them if they notice one's missing. I might have 'accidentally on purpose' smudged the 6 to make it look like a 5 when I spilled my espresso on the paperwork this morning..."

"Arnaud, you're too good at this. What else have you 'saved'?"

"Nothing pépère, this is the first time I've ever done anything as crazy as this."

"OK, against all my good judgment I'll turn a blind eye. Now get it off there *toute de suite*, and I know nothing about this. I was away when you arrived, got it?"

"Got it pépère, thanks so much. So can you give me a hand pushing it into the barn?"

"It doesn't run? It's brand new."

"It doesn't run. Not sure it ever did."

Arnaud had gotten rid of Jacque, got Grand-papa to say yes and now, for the final piece of the puzzle.

"I thought there were six? I swear I'd heard you were hauling six."

"Nope, that's it. That's all of them. I think I overheard one of the foreman say Mr. Citroën himself wanted to keep one at the factory after all, for a museum or something."

"More likely for jaunting around his summer house in the South, I bet."

"Yeah, these rich playboys have the life, don't they? Bet he has a mistress in every dealership."

"Yup, nice life. Let me get these cars off, I'm late for another pick up."

"Why are you late anyway, you were suppose to be here early this morning?"

"Engine problems. She just died on me. Couldn't get it started again. Turned out to be the fuel pump."

FOUND

At each family gathering at the farmhouse Arnaud would head out to the barn with gramps to sneak a look at the 22CV, still under a pile of hay. In the fall of '55 grandfather passed away, carrying the secret to his grave; and Arnaud's father inherited the land.

"Papa, I've got a little secret to tell you. I'm not sure how you're going to take this, but, well, here goes…"

"… *merde*, let's go see it. I don't know what to say," Francois said. "I always wondered why papa steered me away from this pile of hay. I'm still not sure how mad I am but I sure don't like how you both deceived me for so long," he said as they started to pull the hay off the mound. "Seems like papa kept fresh hay on it all these years. These came out in '34, right? That's over 20 years ago!"

After they'd removed enough of the hay they each grabbed a corner of the thick canvas tarp and pulled it slowly back as they walked along opposite sides, from front to back.

"Well, the body looks pretty good, but the interior's been eaten alive," Arnaud said staring at the now non-existent leather.

"They've been feasting for years. I always wondered why we had so many fat mice in here."

They both quickly went to the front and stared at the faired-in headlights and the magical 8 symbol on the majestic grill.

"You know this is by far the rarest Citroën of all time. I've read stories for years about how one or two of the 22's went missing. Some dentist in Brittany supposedly had them. Then there's the story of one in Vietnam needing a water pump but never confirmed. Always thought it was all just lore. But here she sits. In my barn of all places! Now what?"

"I've had over 20 years to think about this dad, so I have a plan. We make it a faux 22CV."

"Pardon?"

"We fake that it's a fake. No one will believe it's real anyway. That way we keep it as is, but find a really early 11CV roadster in a wrecking yard and use its serial plate instead."

"What about the V8 engine?"

GREGORY LONG

"Thought about that too. We could just leave it and never open either hood but that won't work—Gregoire will immediately scuffle under the car and figure out things aren't what they should be. Or, better yet, we get a '34 Ford V8 from America and say we created a replica. We can hide the original engine, which I don't think ever worked anyway. It might actually have been a camouflaged Ford V8 anyway."

"Seems like you're looping me into your life of deceit."

"If you're willing, papa. That way we'll get to drive the real 22CV after all."

"Well life's been getting a tad boring of late son…"

FOUND

9. The Claimer

"So Carlos, tell me if I've got this right as it doesn't sound very smart or practical. You buy an old clunker car and spend a bunch of time and money to soup it up and then go race it at Western Speedway. And if someone wants to buy the engine from you you have to sell it to them for $250."

"Yup. It's called the Claim Rule, and the car is therefore a Claimer. That's why if you use too many fancy expensive parts to get it to go faster then anyone can just come along and 'claim' it from you. Keeps everyone spending similar money and levels the playing field.

"So has anyone ever tried to claim this hunk of junk?"

"No, and that's the last time you get a ride in her."

"I'm just joking, I love this thing. My mum hates the noise though."

"I know I'm not supposed to drive it on Hollydene but I have to tune it up somehow before the race.

"Hey, you like foreign racecars, right? I saw one in a guy's backyard just over by the racetrack. He didn't know what it was, said it had been sitting in someone's garage nearby since the early sixties and — as it was being towed to the dump — he ran out and flagged the driver down. He gave him a few bucks if he'd just dump it off at his house. That was 15 to 20 years ago and he's not done anything with it except push it further into the backyard and it's now under a tree. It's in really rough shape."

"I'd certainly love to check it out in any case."

"Let's go a little early next Saturday before the races."

"OK."

"I don't know what it is. No insignias or anything. No engine. No seats. No wheels. No gauges. No serial plate. And, most importantly, no body."

"So there's basically nothing left. Just a frame?"

"It has brakes, steering, and suspension too."

"I don't have any room for it Carlos; mum will have a fit it I bring home another orphan."

"Don't look at me. My mum is certainly not happy with my Claimer taking up room on the driveway. She hates that thing."

"Well boys, I'm afraid I'm moving and she's going to the dump if you can't save her," the owner said.

"Free?"

"Sure, I guess."

"But it's got to be gone by next Thursday or off she goes on Friday morning."

"OK, I'll find a way to save her."

10. Road Chiefing

October 14th 1956

    Sunny, not that warm. No people. Lots of logs washed up on the beach. Wind. Lots of wind. Did I mention it's sunny? Yes, I did. I like this new land. Arrived in Oregon for the first time today. No problem finding a spot to pull over and set up camp. Right beside the Pacific. Right in the wind, and the sun. I don't miss Lafayette, right now at least. I don't miss Estelle, or Else, either. I have only to worry about how to eat crab without proper utensils. I do have a hammer, and pliers. Should be sufficient. Good thing I bought it cooked from the gent at the dock. Need to melt some butter though. The crabman said it was even more delicious dipped in butter.

October 17th 1956

Still sunny. Everyone mentions the weather. And I mean everyone. I was putting air in the trailer's right tire at the filling station with a green dinosaur as its logo and a little girl — couldn't have been more than five — rode up admiring the trailer and said, "Nice weather we're having, right?"

I asked her where her parents were and she said her name was Rose. I again asked her where her parents were and she said four. I said, again, "Rose, Where. Are. Your. Parents?" And she finally said they were at home. I asked where home was and Rose said, 421 2nd Street.

She asked if she could see in the trailer and I said sure, why not. Rose couldn't get up on the platform to the door so I gave her a boost. She couldn't reach the knob either so I turned it for her. She called from inside and asked if I had anything to eat. I got in the trailer and the door slammed behind me — darn wind. I rooted around in the aluminum drawers looking for some biscuits while Rose jumped on the bed.

'Rose, Rose… where are you,' came a very loud, very angry male voice.

I quickly opened the door and put a face to the very angry male voice.

'You seen a little girl, her bike's out here,' said the very angry male voice.

'Oh yes, Rose? She's in here bouncing on the bed.'

'Rose!'

'Yes Daddy, this nice man is getting me something to eat. Isn't his house little? It has wheels too.'

'Get out here, right now before you get a lickin'!'

'Yes daddy.'

'What the hell are you doing taking a little girl into your trailer anyway, I should call the cops,' the father said.

'Call the cops for all I care. I'm just having a leisurely drive up the Coast. She said she was hungry.'

FOUND

'You're not one of those weirdo's are you?'

'Well, I am a writer, so yes, you could say that.'

He asked me what books I'd written and I told him; but neither *The Sound and the Fury* nor *As I Lay Dying* rang a bell so he, and I, dropped it. He said he didn't read much, well, other than the funnies.

October 21st 1956

I like the mountains too. It's a crater filled with water for Christ-sakes. Had to backtrack a bunch to get here but everyone, and I mean everyone, kept telling me about Crater Lake. It's getting really cold at night so I'll be heading back to the coast soon enough. I'm thoroughly enjoying doing little else than keeping a fire going at night, eating, and drinking.

October 23rd, 1956

I do seem to be drinking a lot. At least that's what the empty bottles keep telling me in the morning. I don't think I'm a big drinker but sometimes, yes, I guess I can be. That's what Estelle and others have told me over the years — but only when I'm in celebratory-mode. Not every day. I'd never get anything coherent down on paper if I drank daily. But I'm out here celebrating. Not sure what. Life I guess. Whatever the hell that means.

October 25th, 1956

I've come to very much appreciate this rolling house. Wouldn't work nearly as well in Oxford though. Too sweltering hot. Hot as pitch, actually. But around Gold Beach it's perfect.

It's getting a little rough around the edges now being over 25 years old. Got it for a song in Redding from a friend of Jason's uncle, cleaned out the cobwebs, hitched it up to a '48 Chrysler I paid too much for due to being seduced by its shiny wood sides.

Jason told me the trailer is a Bowlus, and by the faded markings on the skirts it seems to be called a Road Chief. I bet it was really shiny back in the 30's but now it's dull. Very dull. I do like the sinister little windows on the back. It's very comfortable and I can't tell I'm even pulling it, even up Grants Pass.

October 29th 1956

Still haven't moved on very far up the Coast. Had plans to get into BC and Jasper. Heard a lot about Banff. Don't think that's going to happen though. Worried I'm getting to like this a little too much. I have a new job in Thomas Jefferson's town in the spring so I guess I can't stay too long. And it is now getting colder by the hour.

October 31st 1956

Halloween in Coos Bay. No one knocked on the Bowlus's door. Not that I left a light on. And not that anyone's around here anyway.

I'm enjoying not writing. Not feeling a need to write. A vacation. A true vacation. No one's going to ever read these words anyway, so who cares? Not having to do anything I don't want to do. Sleep all I want. Drink all I want. Eat all the crab I want. And not write, all I want.

November 2nd 1956

Surprised it took only a couple hours to get a bite on selling the woody and the Road Chief from a For Sale sign in the window at the trailer court. Guy from a donkey enthusiasts club called Long Ears wants the Bowlus for a clubhouse or something equally as strange. And I thought I had weird hobbies. I made him a combo deal on the Chrysler that he just couldn't pass up. I guess this was a rather expensive vacation after all.

11. A True 'Sports' Car

"Yes, I think we're the only ones daft enough to *still* do it," Peter stated as we wandered around his office in Malvern Link.

It was 1974 and Carson and I were travelling around Europe in an old dilapidated 2CV truckette with a blue whale painted on its flanks. Perhaps the previous owner just liked big mammals, or disliked krill.

Carson had bought the left hand drive 2CV in Switzerland and it was now parked in front of *The Dorchester* in downtown London right on Park Lane. My dad had slipped the

GREGORY LONG

doorman a few quid to allow us to park it there overnight, amongst the Astons and Daimler limousines.

The next morning we were up early and off — as instructed by the doorman as part of our late night deal — to the Morgan factory.

We pulled off for petrol outside the town of Maidenhead and popped back on the road. We didn't see other cars for a long time until, 'Why is that asshole driving on the wrong side of the road', I yelled at Carson just as we both realized *we* were the assholes driving on the wrong side of the road. Carson swung the large wheel harshly to the left and — in typical 2CV fashion — it felt like we were going to tip over but we just body-rolled into the right, I mean, correct lane.

The rather large bloke coming the other way in his 'rallied-prepped' Escort didn't take too kindly to us being on his side, so had swung around and easily caught up to us. Luckily our accents, a strange little car with foreign plates, and us saying sorry a lot, calmed him down fairly quickly: 'We drive on this side over here. You should be driving a car with the wheel on the proper side so you won't forget again!'

He had a point.

We drove on, into the night, mostly on the left side, until we couldn't see much anymore so pulled the van up into a nice paddock, flipped the front seats around, extended the floor, and went to sleep. Two fairly large brothers barely fit in a 2CV van, but they do.

We awoke to lots of yelling and metal bits hitting our corrugated sides.

'What the bloody hell are you doing here? Do you know where you are?' they yelled.

Opening the little rear doors with oval windows we emerged into the dawn rubbing our eyes. We seemed to have parked right near a crumbling old castle and, what were these irate gentleman carrying, golf clubs?

'You've gone and parked your rubbish little contraption on our golf course. Are you gormless?'

We played the 'brothers from New Zealand card', again, and told them we were lost and had just pulled off the roadway in the middle of the night after almost being in a car wreck and

FOUND

beaten up by a lager lout.

They calmed down, slightly, and said, 'OK, just get the hell off our fairway right now. You're going to cause a backup on the 4th tee. Where are you headed anyway?'

'The Morgan factory in Malvern Link.'

Three of the four in the foursome quickly looked at one of the chaps and said, 'You'd better talk to Nigel, after you get this bloody van off our golf course!'

Seems Nigel had been on a waiting list going on three years now to get his own Morgan started. Nigel said, 'Just give them a nice hello from Nigel Snowden and see if they'll move mine up in the queue please.' And with a wink, he was off whacking at a small white spherical object, swearing.

The factory tour was laid back. We met with Peter Morgan, in his cluttered office. The son of the founder was a very nice, gracious gentleman. Especially considering we were too young disheveled teenagers who weren't about to put any sum of money down on a new Morgan anytime soon. He certainly had a long-term business perspective, or didn't really care if we'd ever order a car given there was a seven-year waiting list at the time.

There were a few roped off areas but it was fine to just pop about, talk to the artisans, look at stuff, touch stuff, basically do whatever you wanted. I was rather thrilled with how they made the frames not knowing anything about woodwork other than the little bookshelf I'd made for my mum in Year 8 woodshop.

'We use ash. It's tough, durable, and doesn't lose its shape when wet. Critical for a British car,' Joe said with a bit of a snort.

'Has anyone ever provided you with the wood to use in their car?'

'I don't believe so but I haven't been here since 1910 either. Intriguing idea though.'

GREGORY LONG

By 1994 I'd squirreled away a few quid and decided to order my very own Morgan. I was now living near San Francisco in Silicon Valley and there was an importer bringing a few in each year. Seemed they had to be propane powered V8's which suited me just fine. I ordered a BRG Plus 8 with black top and tan leather. The waiting list had contracted quite a bit and it was only a year for US delivery.

I rang up Peter Morgan and asked him if he was amenable to me supplying a few pieces of wood that could be used in the car's construction. I reminded him of my visit 20 years prior and my conversation with Joe — who, incidentally was still there doing the same job. Mr. Morgan said sure, and noted that any components would first require thorough evaluation to ensure the quality was there. It was going into a Morgan after all.

12. Do They Really Go Up and Down?

"Honey, really? A what?"
"A Citroën. A Citroën DS."
"Doesn't that mean lemon in French?"
"It's spelt C I T R O E N, not C I T R O N."
"Close enough."
"Well, they're amazing cars and impossible to get in Europe — they took paid orders for 70,000 of them the first week at the Paris Auto show. Seventy thousand! And Executive Motors in San Francisco has one for a pretty good price, as it's a

demonstrator with only 2,000 miles for $2,500. They list for $3,295.

"It's champagne with an aubergine roof, and blue jersey interior."

"Aubergine?"

"Eggplant."

"Eggplant, you mean it has a purple roof?"

"Honestly, I don't know. Dark purple probably."

"Yellow with a purple roof sounds lovely. Mabel just bought a new Chevrolet station wagon, I think she called it a Nomad, last week and it's quite smart in ivory and yellow," Connie said.

"And they supposedly ride like a dream," Paul uttered as if he was carrying on a conversation with himself.

"The Nomad?" Connie said surprisingly.

"No, no, the Citroën. Want to go down to San Francisco and for a test drive? We can take it down Lombard and test the handling on all those curves. And then head over to Cliff House for a candlelit dinner. You love that place."

"You'd take me all the way there for a candlelight dinner? You must be expecting a really fancy car. But I can't dear. I've got a full Saturday planned with my mom and Joanie. But why don't you take Michael? I'm sure he'd love to go."

Michael loved going for car rides with his dad, especially into the hilly city of San Francisco. He was just six but already a rabid car nut and could name them all—both American and those foreign jobs. Michael had heard his dad talk about the new Citroën especially keying in on the fact it went up and down. Michael was beyond excited. They surprisingly scored a parking spot directly in front of 1535 California Street and, there one was, smack dab in the window of the small dealership. And written directly in big bright green letters on the front window it proclaimed, 'Straight from Paris the Amazing DS19!'"

Michael and his dad spent a half-day in the DS. Michael was amazed that it actually did go up and down, and how much room there was for him to play on the back floor as the driveshaft tunnel had been replaced with thick foam under the carpet.

Paul loved it too. It seemed a bit underpowered, and a

FOUND

bit awkward from a standing start, especially on the steep hills; and that gear-changing was very strange. But he loved the handling of the new front wheel drive, the expansive dashboard and, of course—like his son—how it went up and down. Everyone stopped to ask what it was and, of those in the know, all asked whether it did, in fact, really, truly, go up and down.

It did.

He even surprised himself when he said yes to the salesman. He traded in his '48 Studebaker and they arrived home four hours later just as the sun was setting. Michael was sound asleep on the floor of the back seat.

Connie came out and was extremely surprised, and somewhat agitated, to see their new DS. Her husband usually spent months evaluating 'this and that' on every purchase, big or small. And she was usually in the loop, especially on purchases as serious as this. But truth be known she hated that old Studebaker.

"It was the only one available, so I grabbed it.

"Isn't it beautiful," Paul said, who was an industrial designer by trade.

"Beautiful isn't the first adjective that comes to mind, dear. It looks, how shall I say, a bit, weird."

"It's avant-garde. Aerodynamic. It's true *form follows function*. It was designed by the Italian sculpturist Flaminio Bertoni!"

"That's all well and good dear but it still looks a bit, awkward. Why are there lights on the back of the roof? And where is Michael?"

"Come here. Just sit in it. Isn't it glorious?"

"Oh yes, I love the seats. And so much light. Beautiful material. And I love how those little interior lights illuminate the pillars like a theater. Oh, and there's Michael sound asleep—on the floor! Paul, why did you let him sleep on the floor?"

"Jump in the backseat and see for yourself."

"I'm certain I'll learn to love it dear."

She didn't.

He hated to admit it but it just wasn't ready for prime time. It was really a prototype. And he was, unknowingly, a tester. But he also loved it, leaks and all. Connie, 'not so much', especially after it had left her stranded for the umpteen time. He said it must have been her driving but he really knew better.

Paul called the dealer and they said they'd received some technical bulletins and needed to fix or replace a few things — and all would be good. He asked if they had an English workshop manual and when they said yes he had them post him one, together with a parts book, copies of the tech bulletins, and all the required parts: He'd do the upgrades himself. How hard could it be?

Hard.

Eventually, it felt good to know the car intimately — how all the hydraulic components worked by themselves, and as a team. By the late fifties he'd finally got all the gremlins out and had planned to go on their annual trip to New Mexico to visit his in-laws. It was a very long, very hot journey that took them across the Mojave Desert, in August.

The family farm was up a very bumpy, very washed out, very steep road so Paul raised the suspension and they crawled along until they heard a 'thunk' and the car just stopped in its tracks. The engine was running. The hydraulics seemed fine but it wouldn't move, forwards or back.

Luckily they were close to the farmhouse so Connie and the kids walked up and left Paul to fiddle with the car. Paul needed a rag and reached in the trunk and pulled out a beautiful fluffy peach colored towel Connie had recently bought at Nordstrom's. It should have spent its life drying naked women but it would never be the same. Even with *Tide*. They eventually towed the DS behind the tractor the rest of the way before the suspension lost its pressure.

After hours of evaluation Paul and his father-in-law Pete determined a rock must have somehow skirted the fully panned frame under the car and entered where the driveshafts connect to the wheels. And somehow lodged itself in the selector fork, bending it so it would no longer shift. They phoned Citroën headquarters on Wilshire Boulevard in Beverly Hills and miraculously the parts were on hand. Paul and Pete spent the better part of the vacation in the garage fixing the DS. A fact Connie had brought up on many subsequent occasions.

On their way back home Connie noticed a large rock moving on the side of the highway. They turned around to find

FOUND

a Desert Tortoise which Michael nabbed and placed on the comfy back floor. He was christened Tortilla and spent the rest of his life in California.

The same can be said of the DS but under significantly different circumstances.

FOUND

13. The Fire Brigade

"Hurry, over here, help me push these two out back here, fast!" Jimmy yelled at the top of his lungs to his fireman mate George. "No, no, over here, behind the trailer." Sirens and flashing lights bombarded the senses from all directions.

It had become an inferno, fast—out of control by 5:45 in the early evening—most workers had left for the day. Starting suspiciously in the Trim Shop the flames spread throughout a sizeable portion of Browns Lane. The majority of the almost fully-assembled Jaguars in the fire's path were destroyed. However a few rare D-Type's converted to road-going XKSS were saved by the quick work of the few workers who'd remained at the factory that night to catch up on work.

George and Jimmy had somehow—despite all the commotion—successfully hidden both a new D-Type waiting conversion and a finished XKSS in a trailer that, by happenstance, had been sitting beside the workshop. Jimmy quickly hitched the trailer behind their fire brigade van and hauled it down the lane and a few blocks north where he unhitched it, immediately driving back to the factory and returning to fire fighting.

When the fire was finally contained George sauntered over to Jimmy and asked the obvious question: "Where are the cars?"

"Down over on Ted Pitts Lane by Linda's place," Jimmy responded.

"Why so far away? You didn't need to take them there to get 'em out of harm's way."

"The cars were destroyed in the fire, Georgie. Well, they would have certainly been if we hadn't stepped in. The insurance company will pay Jaguar for their losses. We just got ourselves two new racecars, mate."

George thought for a moment, "That's bloody fraud." And that translates into we go to jail for a long time."

"Don't worry so much Georgie, we need to get them out of here. We obviously can't use the fire van to move them again. Who do you know with a lorry that could pull 'em?"

"I don't know anyone. Why don't you just tell the coppers over there and maybe Jaguar will give us something special as a thank you?"

"Yeah, like a button, or an ice cream. These cars are racecars Georgie. They must be worth around 5,000 pounds each. And no one's going to miss them. That's the beauty of this: the perfect situation that's fallen in our laps."

"How the hell are you going to use them then? Who will believe two broke firemen own two new Jaguar racecars? You're daft."

"Quit asking such difficult questions. It's like we just found 10,000 pounds sitting on the ground and you're walking away from the bundle."

"You're an idiot. Bundles of cash, and two new Jaguars,

FOUND

are not comparable."

"I'm out. I know nought about it," George said.

"I can't do this alone you stupid bugger, come on!" Jimmy pleaded as George walked away into the morning mist away from charred automobile hulks.

"I assume you were involved in the fighting of the big fire last night: Anyone hurt?" Karen asked.

"Not as far as I know, but lots of damage and plenty of cars destroyed."

"Why are you here, by the way—you know Gary and I broke up?"

"No I didn't, sorry. I was just wondering if your brother might let me borrow his work lorry?"

"I doubt it but you can ask, he's still in bed upstairs."

"What's in it for me, mate? Why do you need it? I could be sacked for this."

"I need it to pull a trailer that's got some of my mum's household stuff in it."

"What's in it for me?"

"What do you want there to be in it for you?" Jimmy asked.

"Two tickets to the Coventry City football game next weekend. Fish and chips, and all the beer I can carry."

"Ugh, OK."

Luckily the trailer didn't have JAGUAR emblazoned on its sides so Jimmy hustled over to his mum's house and quickly pushed the thoroughbreds into the back garden—after disassembling some fence sections—directly on the grass. Thankfully his parents were away in Aberystwyth for a few days visiting his aunt and uncle.

By early evening it was dark enough to take the trailer back and park it near the portion of the factory that was lost. Hopefully they'd just assume it had been moved somewhat to make way for the firefighting equipment.

But now how to get rid of such obvious automobiles in only a few days?

Table of Cars:

1st Gear: Breakfast
- 1970 BMW 2800 CS Coupe
- 1967 Saab Sonett II

2nd Gear: Lives of Interesting Cars:
1 – 1957 Ferrari 250 Testa Rossa Scaglietti Spyder
2 – 1967 Citroën DS 21 Chapron Décapotable
3 – 1967 Jaguar XK-E Fixed Head Coupe
4 – 1974 Land Rover Series III
5 – 1957 Mercedes Benz 300SL Roadster
6 – 1971 Plymouth Barracuda Convertible
7 – 1950 Tatra Tatraplan T600

3rd Gear: It's a Beautiful Day for a Tatra Hunt
- 1967 BMC Mini Moke
- 1967 Panhard 24BT
- 1968 Buick Wildcat
- 1972 Citroën 2CV
- 2001 Saab 9-3 Viggen

4th Gear: More Lives of Interesting Cars:
8 – 1934 Citroën 22CV Convertible
9 – 1957 Maserati 200Si
10 – 1935 Bowlus Road Chief, Front Kitchen
11 – 1994 Morgan Plus 8
12 – 1956 Citroën DS19
13 – 1957 Jaguar XKSS and 1957 Jaguar D-Type

5th Gear: Lunch

6th Gear: Even More Lives of Interesting Cars:
14 -
15 -
16 -
17 -
18 -
19 -
20 -

FOUND

Overdrive: The Garages of Mr. Brant
 1 - The Roundhouse
 2 - The Crow's Nest
 3 - Brantville

5th Gear:

Lunch

"Your regular table?"

"Regular table? We've only been here together once before," Mr. Brant replied.

"You stayed long enough the first time for it to be worth multiple visits," Doris shot back.

GREGORY LONG

"OK then, we'll have our regular order, Miss Smarty-pants," Tanner quipped with a smile.

"Two corn beef hash dark rye toast two eggs over-easy, Mr. Tasty, please," Doris yelled. "Smarty-pants my ass."

"So what do you do when you're not playing with your family and working at the newspaper?" Mr. Brant asked Tanner.

"I love to play practical jokes on my twin brother. And he likes to play them on me."

"So who was the bigger bully?"

"Neither, we weren't mean, per se, but I did have a big bully in school when I was in elementary school. His name was Murray and to this day he scares the bejesus out of me. He smoked. He swore. He was overweight. And wasn't that smart. The prototypical bully. And one day he spray-painted, in G I A N T letters across the huge exterior gym wall at school: Tanner Loves Sonya. Love at Frist Site. And he spelled it F.R.I.S.T. and S.I.T.E.

"And yes, I was 'into' Sonya. She was the school's blonde bombshell from Sweden — how incredibly exotic for our little town. Of course I'd only told a couple of my friends about my secret crush on her but someone must have told Murray and that was it: Now everyone in the entire school knew because there was only one Tanner, and definitely only one Sonya.

"I was mortified. I turned around and ran home. I didn't know what else to do. I was beyond embarrassed. Thankfully the janitor quickly painted over Murray's questionable artwork but the real damage was done. I don't believe I had to guts to talk to Sonya ever again...

"And if that wasn't enough one day I felt this cold gooey wet stuff on my head. Murray was sitting behind me and had just poured a bottle of rubber cement on my head. I got up, slowly, and sauntered out of the school and ran all the way home, again. By the time I arrived the rubber cement had hardened. Mum had to cut it out of my hair.

"She then called the school and ratted Murray out. I was very worried about the wrath of retribution but he didn't try anything after that. At least to me. He did, however, get caught bullying another kid and was taken to the principal's office for a strapping — yes, even in my day you got strapped with a leather

FOUND

belt if you were bad at school—and, for the record, I never got strapped. The story goes that Murray grabbed the principal's arm as he was about to strap him and broke his arm on the desk. I don't think any of us saw Murray again after that. I heard years later he was in jail. Not surprising."

"Wow, I'm amazed you're as well-adjusted as you seem. OK, I'll bite, what's the best prank you played on your brother?"

"This one cost me a lot of money but was certainly worth the effort.

"Devin had just bought a brand new Chevy pickup truck. He'd saved up forever and finally pulled the trigger. He wouldn't let me near it, let alone drive it, or even get in it. Soon after he brought it home he had to go on a three-week trip to Asia and made me swear to him that I wouldn't touch it. He told his wife Janice to call him—no matter what time of day or night—if I came anywhere near it. So, of course, it was mandatory I do something. Something evil.

"Three weeks was barely enough time but I was finally able to locate the identical truck, in the same white colour as his, that had been totaled in an accident—it had been hit in the back, and forced into the car in front of it. Accordioned, I think they call it. Luckily the body style had been around for a few years and, being white, a typical construction vehicle colour, it was now only next to impossible to find versus impossible. So, I bought it and had it flat-bedded to his house. Janice thought it was hilarious so immediately gave me the keys to his new truck and we switched them out.

"Devin took a cab home from the airport—there was no way Janice or I could have kept a straight face for the entire ride, so we just hid behind the shrubs between the houses. And so did about 20 others.

"Devin got out of the cab, grabbed his bag from the trunk and—like a movie scene—started walking up to the house and twisted his head ever so slightly to the right to look at his new pride and joy, and just stopped dead mid-stride. His mouth dropped, bag dropped, and he dropped to his knees and let's out the loudest, most blood-curdling T A N N E R ! anyone has—or will ever—hear. His reaction was worth the thousands of bucks this set me back, times ten."

"OK, that didn't happen," Mr. Brant said, enraptured in

the story.

"Well, yes, it did and I have 20 plus witnesses."

"What'd he do?"

"Got up, walked over to it, turned around and stormed into the house, smashing the front door closed behind him. And then he saw mum and dad, a bunch of his friends, and they all yelled, Surprise!

"Devin — now even more confused screamed — 'It's not my birthday!'

"Everyone was smiling and laughing and Devin continued to be totally bewildered. My dad finally said, 'Did you check the license plate on the truck?'

"With that Devin turned around, stormed back out only to find me standing on the truck's roof laughing my proverbial head off. As was everyone else. And when he saw his new truck being driven towards him with our buddy at the wheel he fell on the driveway and laughed so hard, and for so long, I thought he was going to die."

"That is the best story I've ever heard! How'd he get you back?"

"When I went on an all-inclusive vacation cruise for two weeks.

"I was worried about putting on more weight so stupidly told him I was really going to try to hold back. Of course that gave him an idea: our friend Dale is a haberdasher so Devin snuck into my house and borrowed a bunch of the clothes I wear most days for work. My wife Paige was in on the prank so she'd put them aside so he could quickly pick them up. The asshole then took them down to Dale's and had them all taken in an inch or two. Mostly the pants but some suit jackets too. He then enlisted another friend who was able to somehow rig our bathroom scale to consistently register 15 pounds over.

"He then told all our friends and some of my work-mates about the plan and when he picked me up from the airport on Sunday night he casually mentioned that I sure seemed to have packed on a few LB's while I was away.

"When I got out of the shower that first Monday morning back I, sure enough, stood on the scale and was flabbergasted to see I'd put on over well over 10 pounds. Crap! And when I got dressed for work I noticed it was really hard to

FOUND

get my suit pants done up and my jacket was really tight across my stomach. Paige told me afterwards she was smirking behind my back as I waddled out to the car. A couple of guys at work asked me if I'd hit the dessert table a bit too many times or, that those Piña Colada's sure must be fattening. It took me a few days to figure it out and boy was I both mad and impressed."

"So, I guess you're up next then?"

"Yup, and I'm working on it."

"Well if there's anything I can do to help, just let me know."

"I might just do that, thanks," Tanner said. "You don't have a backhoe by any chance do you?"

"OK guys, you're gonna float on out of here. That is, if you actually ever leave," Mr. Tasty joked.

"I know, I know, this young man keeps telling me stories. Good stories. Really good stories."

"As good as your DB Cooper story?" Mr. Tasty joked.

"Well, we probably don't have any as good as that one, right Tanner?"

"Not a chance."

"So what happened to the two hundred grand?" Mr. Tasty asked.

"It's all held up in the courts. I assume the insurance company will get it but who knows—maybe Mr. Brant and I will be able to buy lunch with the proceeds one day."

"But you're so famous now," Mr. Tasty said.

"Don't remind me. We should have just put it all back and run. It's been a madhouse ever since. Oh well, seems to have calmed down a bit now. Have you heard what they're doing with the Tatraplan, Tanner?"

"Nope. But it would be cool if we got first crack at it."

"Dream on," Mr. Brant said. "It's going to go to one of those museums with Elvis's cars."

"So, have I told you my Jay Leno story yet?" Mr. Brant wondered.

GREGORY LONG

"That Jay Leno?"

"Know another?"

"Do tell," Mr. Tasty said as he pulled a chair over to their table.

"It started with an email from my friend Gary saying we'd been invited as a guest of Jay Leno to The Tonight Show, then to his hangar, now automobile garage, to check out his cars and have a BBQ. Gary had helped Jay find an old Alfa he'd been looking for forever, an 8C 2900B as I recall, maybe a Mazda Cosmos, oh I can't remember. And Jay told Gary that if he was ever in LA to look him up. Magically, a few weeks later, we just happened to be in LA.

"As luck would have it I was getting a divorce and moving out of the house the day after the Leno visit was planned. Of course I had to go for it—once in a lifetime opportunity and all.

"I arrived at the airport and my flight was delayed. I'm basically in tears at the counter asking, 'Isn't there anything you can do?' Thankfully, I stayed sort of calm so she took pity on me; found another flight, with a different airline, but the door was closing in 12 minutes. And, of course, it's directly on the other side of the airport. I did 'an OJ' as best as a man my age can 'do an OJ' and made it with literally 15 seconds to spare."

"What's an OJ?" Tanner asked. "You kill a few people and escape with your buddy in a white Bronco?"

"No, smartass. Hertz commercial, oh forget it...

"Gary picked me up at LAX, top down in his pink rental '59 Caddy—proper Beverly Hills style, he said. And we head north to the Burbank's NBC Studios and yes, traffic was just as horrendous as expected. We finally made it, grabbed our tickets, and were personally escorted to phenomenal seats, right up front.

"At the end of Jay's pre-show warm-up he asked the audience, 'Where's my friend Gary?' '*My*' Gary puts up his hand: I'm sitting with a celebrity! After the show wrapped we're escorted on stage to meet Jay; and an NBC photographer takes our picture. Jay then said, "Let me get out of this ill-fitting suit and we'll meet across the street at the Mobil gas station." We followed him in his '66 Oldsmobile Toronado; converted from front to rear wheel drive and something like 1,000 horsepower. Let's just say that Jay 'smoked us' in a race against the old Caddy to his garage."

"He really switched it from front to rear wheel drive?"

"Yup, he just does stuff like that. It's nice to have imagination, creativity, and gobs of money.

"We arrived at the 'World's Largest and Nicest Garage' and Jay had to do an interview for some TV show so we're shown around the huge old hangars by his head mechanic Bernard. Jay certainly has an eclectic interest in cars: a perfectly restored early Saab 96; a collection of steam cars, a '41 fire engine which was the old Warner Bros. 'lot' fire-truck 'thrown out' in the '60s and left at the Burbank airport as a wind shield before it had to be removed post-911; a fine selection of multiple-million dollar Duesenbergs and Pebble Beach-ready Bugatti's; a Fiat Topolino, and his beloved Citroën SM.

"After the tour we met up with Jay again and poured over his newly acquired Tatra T87 while Jay made up some burgers for the BBQ. Yes, Jay was wearing his patented denim on denim look while in the kitchen making patties for us all. We sat around gabbing with our host and a few of his full-time mechanics in his amazing garage kitchen he'd constructed for a Martha Stewart show. We just talked cars, of course, mostly R. Buckminster Fuller's amazing Dymaxion, over root beer and burgers. Just like normal 'car guys'."

"Mr. Tasty, get the hell back there. Your smoke break is working way overtime."

"Yeah, yeah, hold your horses…"

"It was getting late and I had to catch my flight. I asked Jay for directions to LAX and he said why don't you just follow me and when I exit the highway to go home you just continue south to the airport.

"With that, Jay walked over to one of the garages and I asked, 'What car are you going to take?' He responded, 'I don't know yet.' A few minutes later he appeared in a gorgeous ivory early '50s Jaguar XK120, no roof. And I don't mean the roof was down. There was just no roof as best as I could make out anyway. Gotta love California. And the Jag clearly had something done to the motor as it had a very sweet sound. We followed him through the back streets of Burbank and onto

Ventura Highway. And there we were, zooming along, talking, I mean yelling, at each other—Gary and I in our old pink Cadillac convertible and Jay in his Jag. Yes, it was surreal. And certainly a once in a lifetime experience I'll obviously always cherish. And 'that woman' was finally, legally, out of my life to boot!"

"Awesome. Do you stay in touch still… think you can get me in?" Tanner asked.

"Nope, and nope but I'd love to show-off my mechanized marvels to you sometime."

"I'd love nothing better. How about this Sunday, after church?"

"I don't have much interest in church, but sure."

"Perfect, see you then."

Tanner had spent hours with Mr. Brant. He was over 50 years older but clearly kindred spirits. He'd found someone who was as interested in his life, as he was in theirs. The common denominator was interesting cars. The magical part was the dialog—most *car guys* just talk. And talk, and talk, and talk. And most *old guys* just talk. And talk, and talk and talk. It becomes especially irritating when you get into a conversation with *old car guys*: It gets boring really quickly when there's no give and take.

Mr. Brant wasn't like that.

Tanner wasn't like that.

They had wonderful two-way conversations about amazing cars, with a spice of life thrown in for good measure.

Table of Cars:

1st Gear: Breakfast
- 1970 BMW 2800 CS Coupe
- 1967 Saab Sonett II

2nd Gear: Lives of Interesting Cars:
1 – 1957 Ferrari 250 Testa Rossa Scaglietti Spyder
2 – 1967 Citroën DS 21 Chapron Décapotable
3 – 1967 Jaguar XK-E Fixed Head Coupe
4 – 1974 Land Rover Series III
5 – 1957 Mercedes Benz 300SL Roadster
6 – 1971 Plymouth Barracuda Convertible
7 – 1950 Tatra Tatraplan T600

3rd Gear: It's a Beautiful Day for a Tatra Hunt
- 1967 BMC Mini Moke
- 1967 Panhard 24BT
- 1968 Buick Wildcat
- 1972 Citroën 2CV
- 2001 Saab 9-3 Viggen

4th Gear: More Lives of Interesting Cars:
8 – 1934 Citroën 22CV Convertible
9 – 1957 Maserati 200Si
10 – 1935 Bowlus Road Chief, Front Kitchen
11 – 1994 Morgan Plus 8
12 – 1956 Citroën DS19
13 – 1957 Jaguar XKSS and 1957 Jaguar D-Type

5th Gear: Lunch
- 2002 Chevrolet Silverado 1500 Regular Cab
- 1953 Jaguar XK120 Drop Head Coupe

6th Gear: Even More Lives of Interesting Cars:
14 -
15 -
16 -
17 -

18 -
19 -
20 -

Overdrive: The Garages of Mr. Brant
1 - The Roundhouse
2 - The Crow's Nest
3 - Brantville

6th Gear:

Even More Lives of Interesting Cars

FOUND

14. Z is for Zagato

Erik wanted something small, fast, and very beautiful. He'd just finished law school and was now articling in Vancouver. He wanted to give himself a present for getting through all those exhausting years of late nights, late coffee, and late papers.

Of course he couldn't afford it but that's what loans were for. And the fact his grandfather had slipped him $2,500 and told him to do something special for himself didn't hurt either.

Gramps was from the old country, Sicily to be exact; had

come over after the war with nothing, and had made a great living growing, of all things, daffodils. Little did he know Vancouver would be a great place to grow them and that the land he was growing them on would one day be worth a fortune.

Luigi didn't want to spoil his grandson but he also didn't want to die with a ton of money either—he wanted to spread it around to those grandchildren who'd proven they had good heads on their shoulders combined with a healthy work ethic. Erik passed muster on both counts.

Erik had spent summers with his other grandparents back in Italy and had fallen in love with both Italian girls and Italian cars. His first love, in the car department, was Ferrari, of course, but he'd need to be a big-time lawyer one day before he could ever afford one of those. Same thing for a Maserati or Lamborghini.

He'd come to love Fiats, Alfas, Lancias, especially the Abarth versions. He'd briefly toyed too with the likes of Karmann Ghia's, 356's, MG's, Triumphs but was hooked on Italian—mainly because of his roots. And the fact they handled great. And sounded great too.

After lots of test drives and reading everything he could get his hands on Erik walked into *Pacific Italia Auto* on Powell and splurged on a new 1961 Alfa Romeo Giulietta Sprint Zagato in Mayflower White with a blood red interior. It made both him, and nonno, very happy.

The car finally arrived and was everything he'd dreamed of but it just wouldn't stop overheating. The dealer tried changing out almost everything in an attempt to remedy it but Erik eventually became very frustrated and disenchanted with it.

He did become very enchanted, however, with another Italian import, Dani Acardi. They married in March. Erik had calculated it would be cold enough outside to use the Zagato as their wedding get-away car as they were staying close-by at the *Hotel Vancouver*.

By this time in his life he was starting to make a few bucks, had bought an impressive piece of land cheap from his grandfather, and built a nice glass-filled 60's home with a

FOUND

dynamite view of the harbour. When he finished the garage he just pushed the Alfa in the back, covered it up, and never used it again.

Surprisingly to the dealer—and almost everyone else—he'd found a little-raced Giulia TZ he thoroughly enjoyed for many years before it rusted away in front of his eyes.

FOUND

15. Worse Than a Car Crash

Adam had amassed a huge valuable collection. His prize possessions ranged from a James Bond DB5, an original Batmobile, to a BMW 507 and a Toyota 2000GT.

Adam had grown up in a lower-middle class family in Eastern Washington's, Pullman. His dad was a janitor at Washington State University and his mom a cafeteria lady there. Pullman was a pure college town. If you didn't work at *WSU* you were probably a wheat or cattle farmer.

He'd spent his entire life in Pullman. Gray and crimson ran through his veins. It shocked himself — and everybody else in town—when he accepted a position as a wide receiver at archrival UW. Adam had worked extremely hard in school at both academics and athletics. The 'smarts' part of the equation didn't come as easy to him—he was someone who had to work hard to get great marks. Football was another thing though. Adam had an uncanny natural ability from a very early age. Whacking the ball off the tee at four; Bending it like Beckham at seven; and running a 100m dash in 13.1 at twelve.

But he had always dreamt of being a *Coug*. Now he was on his way to being a *Dawg*, a Husky dog.

After a very successful first year where he broke all the existing records, Adam went out for a pass and spectacularly caught the ball in the air with just one hand. He wasn't grandstanding, really, it just felt right to catch it that way. He knew he'd get an earful from Coach even though he'd successfully caught it. But when he came down, trying to ensure his feet were within the sideline, his left ankle just shattered. The doctors said it was worse than a car crash—they'd never seen anything like it.

A very close call with Compression Syndrome and losing his leg forever if his mother hadn't got him back to the hospital in time. Numerous serious operations; and 12 titanium pins caused him to hang up his cleats. Adam still spent tons of time with the team, on and off the field, as he healed.

Turned out, thankfully, he found another love. Two actually. First was Traci who he'd met at *WSU*. And writing software. There were a ton of great paying jobs all around Seattle with Mr. Gates' Microsoft being founded there and a newcomer called Amazon.com which labeled itself as 'The World's Largest Bookstore'. The internet was starting to radically change many businesses like Amazon was doing to book retailing and Adam wanted a piece of this brave new world. After a few small scale flops Adam hit upon the idea of screen savers. Computer screens that were left on could burn the image of what was last on the screen. If you moved things around while it wasn't being used you'd save the screen. Early examples were wonderfully nerdy images dreamt up by the developers themselves and they just gave them away for free.

Adam thought about how valuable that real estate was

FOUND

in terms of advertising space and prototyped a system that could pull in and display ads. Advertisers loved it. Users didn't. They were inundated with ads all day long. They loved that the typical computer was a refuge from the constant onslaught by marketers. Adam continued to iterate and thought about what would users actually want to see on their computer screens: What would they look forward to seeing each day?

Relatively low-cost digital cameras were just starting to appear even though the resolution was poor but it allowed users to have digital picture frames. And also people loved to look at high-resolution images of nature, fancy cars—whatever they were 'into'. But everyone could just add those themselves, what 'value-add' could Adam's start-up provide?

It was during this period that Adam's acquisition of cars subsided somewhat. eBay was just starting up and offering cars so it was very easy to browse, and fantasize about getting this one or that; but he kept his focus, and his bank account on the digital world.

One crisp and cloudy January morning Adam was walking along Boren Street and popped into a knick-knack shop to pick up something small for his wife's birthday. He'd already gotten the 'big gift' but wanted there to be more than one present. He spied a calendar on a table—but not the typical one you hang on a wall—one you tore off the top of each day of the year. There were all sorts to choose from: humorous ones featuring well-known comics, some that gave a 'new word of the day', and others that provided pithy motivational pick-me-ups. He loved the *Far Side* edition and knew Traci would too.

It took a few days sitting on the front hall table before the inspiration came to him: He looked forward to tearing off the previous day's comic to unearth the new one each morning as he headed out the door—if Traci hadn't gotten there first—and thought, why don't you get a new comic each day on your computer? It can move around the screen once in awhile to reduce burn-in? A few weeks later he'd met Mr. Larson's publisher and eventually struck a deal.

And, all of a sudden it seemed everyone wanted a funny screensaver. He was certainly onto something. And also to becoming a very wealthy young man.

As his net-worth increased, so did his purchase of more cars. Traci mentioned on more than a few occasions that they were spending a lot of money on them but Adam reassured her that they were investments.

'Not an expense,' he would say. 'An asset, mark my words honey.'

Traci would continually fret about where they were going to put them all; and what about insurance costs? But the really weird thing about the obsession was that he wouldn't even let his three-year-old twins anywhere near them. He was panicked they'd somehow harm his 'other' babies. That was the last straw, Traci told him one night after noticing he was spending far too much time perusing eBay.

'Adam, you're obsessed. You've gone overboard,' she told him in a calm but firm voice, while sitting beside him on the computer.

'Just two more, honey and I'm done.'

'Really, truly?'

'Yes,' he responded. 'The hunt is almost over.'

Ten days later he was finished. What he'd started so many years ago in Pullman was finally complete.

FOUND

16. Black Sea Road Tripping

"Take it. We have orders to take whatever we *want*, I mean, *need*."

The '35 Tatra T77 had been stopped at a checkpoint and was immediately commandeered as a staff car for the Third Reich. The new driver had heard the stories of Tatras being notoriously dangerous in the curves — with its air-cooled V8 3.4 litre engine hanging out over the back wheels — but it was so fascinating, so magnificent he just had to have it. It was also the limousine version complete with resplendent burgundy leather, and a sliding glass partition, so he was sure his bosses would like it too.

Hans Ledwinka had created a couple of aerodynamic masterpieces just before the war and they'd become highly prized by the invading forces. Ledwinka had leveraged Paul Jaray's work on the Graf Zeppelin dirigibles, and then in automotive design with Tatra Werks licensing relevant Jaray patents and design proposals. The first was the T77 of '34 followed by the T77a, and T87.

But this was an original T77. Not the tamer and more tractable T87. The T77 was longer, wider, and had a coefficient of drag of only 0.212 — unheard of even to this day. The car became a favorite of Dr. Eugen Heydrich, the Deputy Reich Protector of Bohemia and Moravia, who used it on 'official' and 'unofficial' business throughout Czechoslovakia, before it somehow found its way into Leningrad, just before the war ended. These so-called spoils of war were auctioned off and — as all the cars were lined up with their hoods open for inspection — the Tatra was passed-by as thought to be engine-less. A middle-aged man, Vlad Babkin, peaked around the back, lifted the enormous finned lid and gazed upon its impressive magnesium-alloy V8 power-plant. Mr. Babkin bought the Tatra personally, a rather rare event in Russia, and used it mainly for summer trips with his family to the Black Sea. It wasn't long before he locked it away in his shed forever, worried it could be repossessed by the authorities as they cracked down on private ownership, especially of such a grand, flamboyant automobile.

17. Dairy Freeze

A 1956 356 Carrera GS/GT Speedster has always been a rare beast. And temperamental, but that fall morning at the racetrack she looked amazing in her bright white paint, tiny windshield, and numbers on its side.

"I'm so tired of it never keeping its tune, burning oil, and no one knowing how to fix it. Just take the bloody thing out and be done with it. Its racing days are over anyway," Jim said irritably.

"I've got a good 1600 I can put in instead if you want. Give me the 4 cam and $500 and I'll put it in for you."

"You'll give me a good engine for a bad engine?"
"Will do."
"Why?"
"Carrera engines are faster but much more finicky, as you're well aware. And I want to one day build the fastest Beetle out there — and this is how I'll do it."
"OK, sounds good to me."

Twenty-five years later James noticed what he just knew had to be a Beetle under the orange tarp sitting behind the Dairy Freeze in Lake Oswego. He walked over, flipped up the corner and, sure enough, it was a black Bug and, by the looks of the heart taillights, was an early oval. It seemed to be all there but pretty beat up and looked to have been tricked out to be a street rod or something. James noticed its factory fabric sunroof and immediately had to have it.

"Hi, I'll have a dipped cone and a '56 Beetle please," James said to the young sweetheart behind the counter.
"Excuse me?" she asked.
"Do you know anything about that VW in the back with the lovely tarp on it?"
"Oh yeah, that eyesore belongs to one of the cooks that used to work here, Kenny Jones."
"Used to work here?"
"Yes, left in a huff a few months back and we haven't seen hide nor hair of him since."
"Why's the car still there then?"
"I don't know. Dan, can you come up here," she yelled.
Dan waddled his way from the smoky office in the back with a Matinee cigarette between his first and second fingers. "What can I do ya for," he asked James as he sorted out the counter's salt and pepper shakers.
"I'm just an old VW guy and wondering what's going on with that one in the back?"
"You're the third guy this month to ask about that piece of junk. It's not for sale. Some A-hole left me high and dry on a stifling hot day at 4pm just as things were starting to hop. I had to man the stoves all night by myself. Haven't heard from him ever since, and I hope I never do.

FOUND

"How long ago was that Kellyanne?"

"Huh?"

"How long since that bastard Kenny left?"

"It was summer right and it's January now so I guess close to 6 months."

"Well after six months you can sell the car you know. You just have to charge him reasonable storage and then try to tell him that he has to pay up and take the car, or you get to take the car. DMV can verify all this."

"You think I have time to verify anything at the bloody DMV? Are you crazy?"

"Do you mind if I at least look at it a bit more thoroughly?"

"Depends. What are you buying for lunch?"

"A dipped cone," then a long pause, "and a cheeseburger, large fries and a Coke."

"What size Coke?"

"The biggest you have."

"OK, but don't rip anything off or I'll have your balls cut off."

"Dan, you're such a pig," Kellyanne said in her usual pissed off tone.

James grabbed his grub and checked out the Bug. It looked fairly good actually. Pan wasn't too bad. Had some nice gauges, and a high-end shifter. He went around the back and strangely enough the trunk lid had a lock on it. Damn, he thought to himself while peering under the back after throwing down some cardboard.

But that didn't look like a typical Beetle engine. I need to get that lid up, he thought to himself. Rooting around in the glovebox he miraculously came across a key with the VW logo on it that fit, and opened the lid. James was all of a sudden peering at the Holy Grail: A 4 cam early Carrera engine. He'd only read about them but here, in the back of a crappy Dairy Freeze in the middle of nowhere, he was actually gazing at one.

He quickly, and gingerly, placed the lid back down, locked it back up while placing the key in his pocket, pulled the tarp back over, and darted back inside.

"You again," Dan snorted.

"Yup, great burger, thanks."

"Yeah, yeah, what do you want now?"

"How about I do all the legwork with the DMV and try to contact Kenny. You don't have to lift a finger; and I either give you a nice chunk of change or you never see me again. It's a win-win for you either way."

"As long as I don't see Kenny around here again either."

"OK, deal."

James never located Kenny—not that he ever looked—so, after giving Dan $600 'sort of legally' he took ownership of the Oval and, more importantly, its magical engine.

18. The Three-Eyed Wonder

"No, no, I'll grab it for you."

"Got anything interesting in there?" Reece asked sheepishly.

"Nope. Wait outside here while I nab it."

"Sorry about the window," Reece said as Bill emerged from the dark garage with an old baseball. Reece wasn't really sorry at all given he'd purposely thrown it through the window at point blank range.

"Why are you throwing a baseball around here anyway? You know I don't like you and your hoodlum friends playing here without asking me first."

"Can I play around here?" Reece said trying not to be too much of a smartass.

"No! And you owe me $20 for the window," Bill said knowing what his reaction would be.

"Twenty bucks! Really, twenty bucks just for a window? I don't have twenty bucks."

"Well I'm sure your mom or dad does. What's your name again?"

Reece was going to say Eddie Haskell but thought the better of it. "Reece. Reece Radisson. I live just down the road and one street over on 4th. My mom Lisa knows your daughter Gina."

"Whatever, just bring twenty bucks over and leave it in an envelope in the mailbox, addressed to me, Bill Waters."

"So, you don't have a special car in that shed," Reece asked sheepishly. "My parents, who were kids back then, say they saw a car with three headlights turn down your driveway but never come out again. And you never open that garage door up. Never. I've been watching for years now."

"It's not a car, it's a spaceship. From Pluto. Took it out only last night for a joyride. Picked up a couple of Martians on my way back but they're in the house now having a cool glass of sarsaparilla, playing euchre. Now get on your fancy Schwinn and don't bring any more sports equipment on my property again."

Bill had spent decades keeping prying eyes out of his garage. Whose business was it to know if he did, or did not, have a car with a superfluous headlight in there?

And, of course, he did.

In 1952, at 35 years old, Bill saw the car at a local supermarket and waited to ask the owner if it could really go in reverse. The guy called him a wise-cracker and, of course, confirmed that it could go backwards.

The owner was from Oregon visiting friends in the area and was just plain tired of all the rigmarole of people thinking

FOUND

they're witty by asking whether it really could go in reverse. Or blabbing on and on about the history of the car—how it was a scam and the guy behind it was thrown in jail and was never seen again. Or that the Big Three were conspiring to kill the little guy with his big ideas. There was usually some thread of truth in their telling of the story but didn't these people think the owner would actually know the history of their own car? Oh well, human nature I guess, to spout out about stuff you don't really know much about.

"Want to sell it?" Bill asked fully expecting him to say no.

"Sure."

"Really? How much?"

"Your truck and a grand."

"My truck and $250. We both know it's out of production, no one knows how to work on it, no parts."

"OK, $500."

"Done," Bill said as he thought this had happened far too fast and far too easily.

"You got a title, right?"

"Well, sort of. Lost it."

"Really? How long have you owned it?"

"About two weeks."

"Two weeks? And you're from Oregon, and no title?"

"I'm from California."

"Then why the Oregon plates?"

"I registered it there. That's where my girlfriend lives."

"Hmmm, how about you take my truck and I take the Torpedo, straight trade?"

"OK."

Again Bill thought this was happening far too easily.

Bill signed his truck's title over and knew he was being really stupid. But he just had to have it. He walked once around it, jumped in the driver's seat, reveled at its spaciousness, amazing instrument pod, and wondered if the windshield really would pop out in an accident.

As he came down his street he noticed a bunch of kids hanging out on their bikes—staring at him, rather, staring at the car—as he zoomed down the street and tucked into his driveway, into the garage, and quickly closed the garage door.

GREGORY LONG

As he emerged from the side door those same kids had come down his driveway and were asking him what it was. Luckily it was dark and they hadn't got a great look but one of the boys said, "It looked like it had three headlights and a really wide rear end. Like Marilyn Monroe."

After he shooed the kids away, he went back in to evaluate his prize. The odometer read just 13,622 miles, which seemed reasonable given the perfect condition of the interior. It drove beautifully and the paint was shiny blue. Bill did wonder for a second whether it would reverse out of the garage though.

Over the years Bill had only told his wife Debbie about it and swore her to secrecy. He told her he didn't want gawkers coming around bugging him to see it. He would take it out on rare occasions, but only really late at night, as he'd never registered it. Debbie thought this was all a bit strange as Billy was fairly outgoing and gregarious. But she abided by the rules. Gina, however, just couldn't keep a secret if her life depended on it. She had snuck into the garage a few times when her dad was away and peered under the thick blankets. And there it was. They were right. A shiny blue car with three headlights. She had to tell someone. Jan, her best friend could keep a secret, right?

Luckily Jan couldn't care less. She was much more interested in talking about boys and Barbie's. Over the years Gina just forgot about the garage and that shiny secret car.

A couple years back Bill died suddenly and left everything to Debbie. Gina, by this time an adult herself with a brood of children, asked her mom what she was going to do with the 'secret car'? Debbie shushed her up, "There is no car."

A few months later Debbie's Alzheimer's had taken a turn for the worse and she was taken to an assisted living home and power of attorney was given to Gina. The first thing she did was sneak into the garage. And there it sat. Just like she remembered it so many years before.

Gina called a friend of hers whose husband was a

FOUND

certified car nut. When he opened the garage door and threw off the blankets he just stood there in disbelief. A '48 Tucker Torpedo, in the flesh, looking showroom fresh except for flat tires. Steve jumped inside and noticed it only had 13,642 miles.

He said, a little too quickly, "How much do you want for her?"

"Dream on Steve. You don't think I'm that stupid, right?"

He didn't; and did feel kind of bad. They knew enough that a Tucker was the rarest of the rare and one in this original condition would be worth a king's ransom.

Steve told Gina to call Emerald City Auctions and have them see what they think it's worth.

After picking their three respective chins off the garage floor the auctioneers asked to see the paperwork and Gina said, "I have no idea, feel free to look around."

They did, and turned up nothing. They checked the serial number and quickly determined it was one of just two of the original fifty-one built that was still unaccounted for. Seems like some Californian had legally registered it in Oregon, submitted a lost title declaration but, after that, the trail had gone cold.

As the final hammer came down the Torpedo had made a world record for a Tucker, $2,915,000. And Gina again wondered why her dad had been so secretive—never driving it—for those so many years.

19. Champagne Expedition

I was the fourth of five, making me part of an identical set of quintuplets. Born in Paris, early in 1934, we were destined for a life of intrigue, exploitation, and abject failure. I was christened Quatrième. At the whim of an eccentric, wealthy industrialist with a need for flamboyant adventures, all five of us ended up — as newborns — in Alberta Canada with the ambitious goal of touching the Pacific Ocean. Our father brought along not only us — his prized quintuplets — but cases of fine champagne, Beluga caviar, his wife, his mistress, and a fine French chef.

GREGORY LONG

We left Edmonton in a grand parade as Lieutenant Governor William Walsh bid us all farewell with a champagne toast. Around 100 people, many friends, and many cowboys from the local area, came along at great expense to help us traverse the wilds of Western Canada. We were the lead characters of the cast, with our photos to be splashed across important newspapers around the globe. Everyone from Paris to Punxsutawney would be waiting in great anticipation as we made our way to the west coast. A famous Hollywood director, with full film crew, was even part of the entourage.

It was certainly exciting, at first. But, as the days—and rain—continued, the going went from tough to impossible; and it wasn't long before I realized I'd be the only Quint to come out alive.

20. Corvette Convenience

"Take it out of your pocket and put it up here on the counter," Elliott said in a surprisingly nice tone. "And never, and I mean never, come in here again even if your mom asks you to pick up a quart of milk. If you so much as step an inch into this shop I'll call the cops. Got it?"

"Yes sir," Mikey said as he slinked the Milky Way bar on the counter and ran out the door.

Elliott was amazing at nailing shop-lifters. Every little kid tried it at least once. If Elliott liked the kid, or the parents, he'd go lightly and just tell them to never do it again. And they never did. Others he treated like Mikey. And some he actually called the cops on, first offense.

Elliott had made and saved good money as a plumber but the work was too insulating for him. He needed human interaction. He needed to chat. He wanted to know who was pissed off at whom; who owed who what; and most of all, who was doing whom.

So he'd bought a medium-sized convenience store a few years back. 7-Eleven's hadn't taken over yet and gas stations just sold gas and repaired cars: No, *'would you like milk with that oil change'*?

Elliott also liked to play the ponies, and poker. And had done quite well at both.

In terms of cars he'd always lusted after Vette's. Any Corvette was interesting but while a '53 wasn't speedy, it was rare, and extremely cool. A '54 was almost identical but he had to have a true '53. Scouring the local papers each morning before anyone else, he finally came across an ad for a '53. He asked for the serial number just to make sure but the seller wasn't sure. The car had been sitting for a few years and the seller just wanted to get rid of it.

Elliott arrived, checked out the numbers, confirming it was a genuine '53 — even had its matching numbers engine — so bought it on the spot. It was complete and he even got it running pretty easily. He drove it around a bit, mostly on weekends but usually parked it outside his shop. One night — locking up late after doing paperwork — he came out to find two guys trying to steal it. Elliott immediately screamed at them to get the hell out while swinging around, going back in his store, locking the door behind him, and calling the police but by the time he turned around again, the boys were gone. He happily didn't recognize either of them.

This happened a few more times over the following couple months so he needed to do something: sell the car, or sell the place.

He did neither.

"You want to lose all this valuable floor space and do what?" his carpenter buddy Johnny asked bewildered.

"Put the Vette in a sealed glass box. Just like I said."

FOUND

"Why?"

"Because I said so, that's why. And because I'm tired of worrying about it being stolen; but I don't want to sell it either. This way I can look at it every day."

"You're dumber than I thought."

"Well, can you help me do it, or not?"

"Of course I can but you're going to need a glass-guy too you know."

"Of course I know that."

Elliott's revenue went down about 12% for the first few months but surprisingly ramped back to normal fairly quickly. Seemed people liked to come to the store with the car inside a box. The Corvette sat in its display case for years upon years until Elliott decided to sell the shop and retire to Florida.

"Perfect car for Destin, Elliott," his friend Ernie said.

"Nope, it's too old and, more to the point, I'm too old to be screwing around with an old car. It's served me well; but it needs to stay put. It's not called *Corvette Convenience* for nothing you know."

"Hey, whatever happened to those lawyers from Detroit anyway? I remember them being pretty adamant you didn't use Corvette in the name?"

"I told them it was in reference to the Corvette warship, just like where they stole the name from. Luckily they never actually stepped in the door here to check. That might have made it somewhat harder to argue..."

Table of Cars:

1st Gear: Breakfast
- 1970 BMW 2800 CS Coupe
- 1967 Saab Sonett II

2nd Gear: Lives of Interesting Cars:
1 – 1957 Ferrari 250 Testa Rossa Scaglietti Spyder
2 – 1967 Citroën DS 21 Chapron Décapotable
3 – 1967 Jaguar XK-E Fixed Head Coupe
4 – 1974 Land Rover Series III
5 – 1957 Mercedes Benz 300SL Roadster
6 – 1971 Plymouth Barracuda Convertible
7 – 1950 Tatra Tatraplan T600

3rd Gear: It's a Beautiful Day for a Tatra Hunt
- 1967 BMC Mini Moke
- 1967 Panhard 24BT
- 1968 Buick Wildcat
- 1972 Citroën 2CV
- 2001 Saab 9-3 Viggen

4th Gear: More Lives of Interesting Cars:
8 – 1934 Citroën 22CV Convertible
9 – 1957 Maserati 200Si
10 – 1935 Bowlus Road Chief, Front Kitchen
11 – 1994 Morgan Plus 8
12 – 1956 Citroën DS19
13 – 1957 Jaguar XKSS and 1957 Jaguar D-Type

5th Gear: Lunch
- 2002 Chevrolet Silverado 1500 Regular Cab
- 1953 Jaguar XK120 Drop Head Coupe

6th Gear: Even More Lives of Interesting Cars:
14 – 1961 Alfa Romeo Giulietta Sprint Zagato
15 – 1967 Toyota 2000GT
16 – 1935 Tatra T77a
17 – 1956 Volkswagen Beetle
18 – 1948 Tucker Torpedo

FOUND

19 – 1935 Quinte
20 – 1953 Chevrolet Corvette

Overdrive: The Garages of Mr. Brant
1 - The Roundhouse
2 - The Crow's Nest
3 - Brantville

FOUND

Overdrive:

The Garages of Mr. Brant

Gregory Long

1. The Roundhouse

It felt like Sunday would never come, but it eventually did.

"The Panhard, lovely. You got it all back together I see. Well done."

"Yes, it's running well actually. Probably needs new tires soon. Always something."

"I can't believe you've not told me its color yet..."

"3LM6 Jaune Pamplemousse."

"Yellow, grapefruit?" Mr. Brant said with trepidation. "Lovely!"

"Shall we go for a ride first, or check out my playroom?"

"Definitely the playroom," Tanner quickly responded.

"OK, let's go in this side door," as Mr. Brant pointed to it with his cane. "Incidentally, how does the Panhard do at pulling your diminutive utility trailer?"

"Jealousy will get you nowhere, Mr. Brant."

As they walked through the door Tanner truly realized the level of Mr. Brant's collector status. In front of him were parked — in a huge, double-deep, circular pattern — some of the world's most sought after cars. In the middle, was a huge leather wingback chair on a raised circular platform.

Tanner was immediately overwhelmed. There were literally too many goodies to look at: *Kid in a candy-store.* His eyes darted from this to that, he just couldn't focus.

"I like to come here and think. And enjoy the sights. Grab that chair over there and place it beside mine if you would."

"When did you start collecting? This is such an amazingly — how shall I say — fabulously eclectic collection."

"Years and years ago. I became an architect and found a niche in building ski resorts. Hotels, condos, amazing chalets for the super wealthy. It was good to me and, if I found a car I liked — that had a good story — I bought it. I lost a bunch in the divorces but well, that's certainly not a story I want to bore you with, especially when we're in my sanctuary."

"I thought you didn't go to church," Tanner said with a smirk.

"This is certainly my church, my son. Look around, what's your Rosebud?" Mr. Brant asked wondering if Tanner would understand the reference.

"I couldn't possibly pick a favourite because it's not just the cars I love but the stories behind them."

"They all have stories. That's what I love too. Ok, pick one to start."

"I quickly count about 20 cars and a travel trailer, and an entire wall of boxed Corgi Toys. I have no idea where to start," Tanner said, honestly.

"How about this Chapron décapotable?"

All of sudden the platform began to swivel counter-clockwise a few feet so they were directly facing the rear of the DS.

Gregory Long

"OK, that's just plain amazing," Tanner said with an enormous smile on his face. "You're not the real Dr. Evil, are you?"

"Who?"

"You know, Austin Powers. Spoof on James Bond? He has evil lairs with sharks with lasers on their heads, and chairs that mechanically swivel around."

"I have no idea what you're talking about. But I do adore Bond movies, especially the early ones with the DB5. Anyway, sometimes it pays to be an architect: You can dream up crazy stuff others would never go for.

"But, ah, yes, the Chapron, it came from a woman near Lake Chelan in Central Washington—I think her name was Pinky. Her family gave me an old photo album showing the car being picked up brand new in Paris and driven all around southern France, stopping in at lots of impressive wineries. I bought it from her when she retired to some Caribbean island and just couldn't take it with her. It was tired but had great bones—the DS, not Pinky. Well, now that I think about it, maybe she was tired and had great bones too? We did paint, interior, new roof, went through the engine, and changed the hydraulics over to LHM. A 'second front' Chapron usine convertible, with Citromatic is still the ultimate spec to me.

"Anyway, I was living for a short while in the small town of Crozet in Virginia and left a message for the editor of *Automobile Magazine*—would they like to drive a newly restored Citroën DS21 Chapron convertible from Seattle to Virginia? I had always thought it would be interesting to have an article written about this car, and what better way to evaluate one than it being driven across the USA. And—just as I thought—it made it across with basically no problems. And the journalist, Sam, ended up falling in love.

"With the car," Mr. Brant said, quickly.

"He's such an amazing writer. I was just rereading the article for the umpteenth time yesterday—yes here it is. I'll read you a few passages:"

We ditch the interstate once out of Washington, choosing instead to cross most of the northwest on the more scenic U.S. Route 2. We pass through Idaho consumed with a new game: What Can We

Drive Over and Not Feel Next? At one point, top down, Chaffee crawls into the back seat at 80 mph and stands up, facing rearward, to take a picture. Five seconds later, when we drop into a three-inch-deep section of shaved highway, the station wagon behind us swerves ten feet to the left. Chaffee turns around, genuinely confused.

'What happened?'

'Oh, nothing,' I say. 'I think they thought you were going to fall out.'

'Why?'

'Didn't you see what we just hit?'

'We hit something?'

At one point, drunk with power, we go out of our way to find speed bumps. Crawling brings a slight lift from the car's nose and tail. A 20-mph pace earns a whump and a little pitch up from the hood. Flying across at 45 mph makes the bump disappear.

Yes. Disappear.

Chaffee, high on ride comfort, spends most of barely paved Montana and Wyoming cackling at traffic.

"And this is great:"

Falling into the embrace of the Décap's well-stuffed, softly sprung front seats is like sitting down at the desk of an early-'60s recording studio, something out of A Hard Day's Night or Mad Men. Mysterious, unlabeled pulls and switches beg for you to fiddle with them. The vent controls alone are mesmerizing - gumdrops on sticks, they look like the flap levers on a Cessna.

"Don't you just love Sam's writing…"

Inescapably, the Citroën evokes a feeling. It makes you ache for the comfort of a dark, smoke-filled room, even if you don't smoke. You hover down the highway in a kind of glissade, floating like a Detroit sled of yore but without any of the attendant wallowing, and you think of women in flowing evening dresses. The mood even permeates the act of shifting - the reach from second to third is a distinctly dismissive gesture, as if you are waving the bellboy to take your luggage up to your room at Le Meurice and you are tired of boring people and their boring cars and mon Dieu, you want a glass of wine.

Gregory Long

"I just love the ride of a DS and, come to think of it, I love just about everything about it. We may have started with my favorite, but I'm not certain."

"And that's a real Tucker I assume?" Tanner asked.

"Yes, I recently bought it at an auction in Arizona with my wife. I thought I was nuts when the guy came over and told me what I'd just spent, including some bullcrap buyer's premium. I don't care anymore. I just love looking at it; and I've put more miles on it since I bought it last year than it's had since 1952. Can you imagine someone having this beauty and never driving it all those decades? I wonder why? Very strange."

"A Tatra of course, that's sure an early one. That fin and those louvers are amazing! I can't believe you've kept this secret from me all this time, especially with all the hoopla around DB's Tatraplan," Tanner said.

"I do like to keep secrets, that's true. But that Tatra is especially amazing actually. I bought it years ago from a Dr. Duehring in Germany. He had a whole barn full of the aerodynamic Tatras. We called them the Fifteen Fins of Dr. Duehring. He even had a T97 — the precursor to the Beetle. I'm sure you've heard the story of Ferry Porsche *'borrowing'* ideas from his classmate Hans Ledwinka to create the Beetle for Hitler?"

"Sort of, something about Ferry looking over the shoulder as Hans' designed a backbone frame, independently suspended, rear air cooled car, with a very rounded body?"

"That's it. Volkswagen paid Tatra handsomely in the 60's when they proved their IP had been stolen but that was long after Mr. Ledwinka had been thrown in jail for helping the Nazis, and died. Poor man. That's a T77, the first truly original serially-produced aerodynamically designed automobile. Dr. Duehring had told me a story of him getting it out of Russia on a covered truck, complete with armed guards, and lots of cash—even though all the export paperwork had been properly completed. Supposedly an individual was able to buy it in the fifties because somebody thought it was missing its engine. Something like that...

"Today, its most nerve-wracking event is getting my relative's brides to the church on time—it is truly the world's ultimate limousine."

"That Cobra is the one I met my second wife in. I'd landed a big contract and just had to splurge. I love European cars but also loved the rumble of a proper American V8. There was a bunch of contenders in 1965 which, incidentally, is my favorite overall year for cars: big engines, tiny engines, no pollution control."

"... or safety features," Tanner interjected.

"True—we had mostly bad brakes, bad steering, bad suspension and tires, bad mileage... and it was an astonishing time!

"I remember trying to decided between a new '65 LT1 Sting Ray coupe in blue, a Ford Cobra 289 in black, a Shelby 350 in white with blue stripes, a red Cheetah, or a yellow Intermeccanica Apollo 5000GT. As you can see I smartly—and with a bit of luck—landed on the Cobra. I almost traded it in on a 427 version in 1967 but after driving one I just preferred the power delivery and handling of the smaller 289. The one time the maxim "no replacement for displacement' didn't hold true, at least for me.

"I vividly remember picking her up at the Shelby factory near LAX. Just walked in, told the receptionist I was there to pick up my new car and she just yelled back, 'Carroll, there's a guy here to pick up his new Cobra.'

"My idol then appeared and acted like we'd been friends forever. We wandered around the shop and finally arrived at my car. Gorgeous black with red interior. That lovely

California black plate with yellow lettering shone brightly back at me, just like today."

"Simple, but lethal. Has it been repainted?" Tanner asked.

"Nope, all original paint, leather, everything but tires which I still have in a back shed out of the sunlight. I remember noticing that a small chrome rollbar had been installed and mentioned to Carroll that I hadn't ordered one. He said he liked to put them on and apologized for not asking first.

He then said, 'No charge, of course.'

"He rarely delivered cars personally but I think he was really enjoying himself telling me all about it. A lot of people have Carroll's signature on their glovebox door but I have photos of him handing me the keys while seated in that very car. I signed all the paperwork and blasted off through LA to Malibu for a celebratory swim in the blue Pacific.

"Returning to the Cobra there was an extremely attractive young lady looking the spitting image—or is it splitting image—I never know, anyway, she looked just like Jane Fonda sitting in the driver's seat wearing an *itsy bitsy teenie weenie polka dot bikini*, with her hands on that very wooden steering wheel.

"'Hello,' she said. 'Nice car. Want to go for a... ride?'

"And that, my boy, was the start of a very disastrous relationship."

"Do tell more," Tanner asked sheepishly.

"Nope. Next."

"Is that an Airstream? It's like a giant rolling mirror," Tanner said as they spun another notch over.

"Nope, it's a 1935 Bowlus Road Chief, front kitchen. It was lovingly restored by a guy up in Canada. Took him the better part of a decade, part-time mind you. It's not easy—there's not a straight line in the whole thing, inside or out.

"Don't you just love it? Isn't it just stunning? It is the embodiment of Streamline Moderne. And it's not just its look and style but it's outrageous dedication to being lightweight. It was the precursor to the Airstream. Story goes that Hawley, not Harley, Bowlus went from designing and building sailplanes for the Air Force to building the *Spirit of St Louis* for Lindbergh. And then lightweight aerodynamic aluminum trailers in the mid '30s. Ended up building less than a 100 until he went bust and legend says Wally Byam then scooped up what was left. Wally moved the door from the front to the side and basically recreated the Road Chief but with a heavier frame. Called it an Airstream; and was the one who made a fortune.

"When John, the restorer, was tearing it apart to redo the interior he found a little diary under the bed in the back. The writer of the diary was one Will F. A little digging and he confirmed a certain Will F did have a solo vacation in Oregon in late '56 with an old trailer before he went off to UVA to be a Writer-in-Residence. Will F turned out to be none other than William Faulkner. As you may know Faulkner won both a Nobel Prize for Literature, and a Pulitzer. How's that for a little bit of Americana? The Smithsonian is interested in the diary, and the trailer, but they're both staying together right here, for now anyway."

"You still have his diary? Hand-written, I assume?" Tanner asked excitedly.

"Yup, I placed it, gingerly, back under the bed in the back of the Bowlus, just where John found it and, I guess, where Mr. Faulkner felt it should reside. And, funny thing is, I seem to do my best writing in there now," Mr. Brant said, with a wink.

"And it looks like you have just the vehicle to pull it. What a great looking 88."

"Yup, got that years ago. I was looking for a Land Rover because my son Carter had used one in his summer job with the BC Forestry."

"Tell me about Carter."

"He's in his late forties now, married with a brood of wonderfully loud kids. They live in a little town called China, in Maine. Sad thing is he drives a Toyota Camry and his wife drives, big surprise, a Subaru. Lovely people. Fine automobiles;

but he couldn't care less about cars. He's into music and is a phenomenal guitarist. Loves sports, mostly football. I don't have a musical note in my body and still can't throw a spiral if my life depended on it. Seems like we all have different genes after all. I even use to have a gorgeous Amphicar in Fjord Green with crazy Apricot seats that we used to plunge into the pond out front and he still didn't catch the car bug. If an Amphicar doesn't snare you, nothin' will."

"Did you read about President Johnson's Amphicar?" Tanner asked.

"Yes, something about him having one but no particular event," Mr. Brant replied.

"Supposedly he'd go for a drive on his ranch in Texas with any new secret service agent, feign bad brakes, and zoom right into his lake. He'd secretly be watching how the newbie reacted: Did he try to save himself, or the President? Not sure if there's much truth to that but it makes a great story."

"It sure does, anyway, where were we? Oh, yes, Carter's Land Rover. A few calls around to the local clubs and I was directed to a place in Ballard who'd catered to old Landies for years. There seemed to be every model, year, and color stacked deep, covering every square inch of available space. And then I noticed a very faded red one pushed up against the fence, piled full of crap. Good crap, mind you. Lots of spare parts. Stuff like that. And sure enough there was the faint outline of an old oval sticker on the door just like all the BCFS trucks sported. I looked inside and it was certainly crusty. But what were the chances it was the actual Rover he'd escaped from being eaten alive in?"

"What?" Tanner yelled.

"I asked the owner of the shop and he confirmed it was an old Forest Service Rover and that it even wore its original red paint. They didn't import many in red, he said, mostly tan and a couple shades of green and a blue. I asked if he wouldn't mind if I checked out its squirter bottle.

"'First time I've ever heard that particular request when looking at an old car but, sure, knock yourself out', Karl said. I think his name was Karl anyway.

"And, while I couldn't be certain it was 'the' one I did notice the bracket was pretty mangled up and Karl said 'Well, look at that, first one I've ever seen with a bad bottle holder.'

"'I'll take it', I said without a second thought."

"And? What about the part about almost being eaten alive?!" Tanner said in disbelief.

"Oh yeah, I'll tell you about that later. It's a good story though, I guarantee it."

"OK then, next!

"It's kind of weird for you to have the king of the heap of muscle cars in here too. It's super rare and special but you seem more of a European car guy to me. It's a '71 'Cuda with a hemi I bet, in Plum Crazy DBC 2210, of course." Tanner said.

"Yup. I just love its sound, looks and, yes, rarity. It's another sad story though. That one originally came from BC and was a 50th birthday present to her husband near Seattle. He kept it perfect; their kids weren't even allowed in the garage where it was parked. But one Christmas Day his friend came over and asked to take his son for a ride to show him what all the fuss was about around a Hemi. The owner checked the oil, got into some unrelated conversation as the engine warmed up, backed out of the driveway and screeched off down the street with tire smoke billowing everywhere... until the hood flew up, hitting the windshield and mangling it up completely. He'd forgotten to the put the hood-pins back in and the air caught it in such a way it just flipped it up and over. Story goes he was so devastated—and embarrassed—he pulled the hood back down, got up on it and flattened it out with his feet enough to drive home. Once he got back he turned it off, threw blankets over it, and never drove it again. I found it—of all places—on Craigslist. I zoomed up and bought it on the spot. It took a ton of expertise but my awesome painter Ken matched the original paint perfectly on an NOS hood I'd found. Ken even matched the factory orange peel. Amazing."

"I'm assuming you know what those are worth now, right?"

"Not really. I know it was a million dollar car for a while but Mopars got kicked in the ass in the so-called Great Recession so I'm not sure where it sits now. It does have the right equipment, and color, and is almost 100% original, except for the hood, of course. Incidentally the original mangled hood is hanging over there. I showed the 'Cuda at the LeMay Museum in Tacoma—the fancy new one, not the old original one Harold had which I prefer because it's not as spic and span. I certainly appreciate the architecture of the new one though, it's gorgeous—I had them hang the s'munched hood on the wall behind the car. People would come up, scratching their heads."

"How sad for the original owner though. To have that monster and rarely use it. How much did he drive it? Do you remember the mileage?"

"I think it has less than 5,000. Have a look."

"Much less. Only 1,853 miles, wow."

"And that looks like a giant car deodorizer over there?" Tanner said.

"Certainly is. It's a very big *Little Tree*. I wear it for Halloween but it's getting a bit ho hum given I've worn it to too many parties over the years. Please borrow it next October. You will make Keira so happy."

"Anything to make a wife happy. You know the saying…"

"No I don't."

"*Happy wife, happy life.*"

"Yes, that's good. I like that… OK now onto the one of my other favorite convertibles.

"I saw an ad in the back of *Road & Track* in the mid-70's for this 300SL. I was always aware of them but your playboy Prime Minister at the time was robbing the cradle while zipping around in his 300SL convertible and Pierre's escapades tweaked my interest again. *Road & Track* was such a great place back then to drool over the cars advertised on their back pages. Used ones were a lot of money even then but it's been a phenomenal unplanned investment. Some people like to watch stocks go up and down; I like to sit here and stare at my mobile portfolio. And it's tough to four-wheel drift a stock certificate or find the perfect line for the corkscrew at *Laguna Seca* driving an oil painting.

"A decade or so back I got a call from a guy in Oregon who'd ordered the car new. Seems he still had the original hardtop and asked me if I was interested. I said not really at first as I'd never thought to drive it in inclement weather but soon realized they should really be reunited. And, as you can see, I think it looks smart with the hardtop on so I usually just leave it like that. That top has some terrific detailing."

"Why do you have some of the cars parked facing out, and others facing in?"

"I switch it up occasionally but typically face the end I like best towards the center. And I love the rear end of a 300SL — it's so darn meaty.

"I had long chat with the original owner and he brought up a great number of amazing photos of when the car was brand new. I especially liked one at the dealership with what looks like the entire staff waving out front."

"He came up here?"

"Yes, he delivered the hardtop personally in the back of a friend's pickup truck. He was dying to see the 300. We took it out and I let him drive it again. He told me he had to sell it when it was almost new because a new baby was on the way. I asked him whether it was a fair trade.

"He just smiled."

"And I bet you smiled when you scored this extremely hot redhead?"

"Not really. I paid what I thought was insane money back in '82 for that machine but it just kept getting crazier and crazier. Even withstood the Black Monday crash of 1987 when the stock market plummeted close to 25% in a couple weeks. Then Enzo's death caused more hyperbolic valuations and things didn't cool down until the Japan's Nikkei crashed in '89. I remembered being offered $2 million for it and turning it down. In 1991 I thought I was the biggest idiot ever. I don't feel that way anymore. The only car I could have done better on was probably a GTO which I stupidly passed on and that *Pink Floyd* guy got it."

"So where'd you get the Testa Rossa?"

"At a track event at the *Seattle International Raceway* — it was still being campaigned by a doctor who'd bought it for just $4,000 back in the mid sixties. And that was a lot of money back then for just an old spent racecar. It was in boxes, had no crankshaft, and its beautiful body had been smashed up fairly badly. He put it all back together himself after having a new crankshaft custom-made in England. It's a beast to drive, but unbelievably satisfying when you get it right. Don't you just love how it still wears its racing livery and looks nicely worn-in? The Pebble Beach types call that 'patina'. I call it 'nicely f'ed up'. And I like my old racecars 'nicely f'ed up.' Keira told me I had to stop using the F-word…"

"And speaking of more than nicely f'ed up. What's the rolling frame over there?"

"That one I found on eBay not that long ago. It had a *Buy It Now* price of $2,500 and it was under Cars & Truck >> Other Makes. It had only been up for 10 minutes when I luckily came across it and immediately noticed it was a rolling chassis of one of my favorite racecars of all time, the Maserati 200Si.

"I thought it had to be a scam as the seller had no rating on eBay yet but I hit the Buy button immediately without thinking a second longer. If it were a scam I wouldn't pay; and, if real, I was a genius. Turns out, thankfully, I was a genius. The car had passed through a number of people and had been kept from being thrown away on numerous occasions. The current owner was losing his storage and thought he had thrown a crazy figure on it. Luckily it was fairly close by so I drove right over, handed him the cash, had him give me a signed bill of sale, and took the pieces away. I've decided I'm too tired now to try to find, build, and assemble all the missing bits to bring it back to its amazing original self. I do like looking at it just like this too though."

"Hey why does your BMW appeal to you, Mr. Brant?"

"Mostly the design. I just love the Hofmeister kink. And the engine and handling are great too. Why do you ask?"

"Oh, don't get me wrong, I've always loved that series, in fact other than the 507, it's my favourite BMW."

"Thank you for not saying Bimmer, or Beamer."

"You're welcome. I just expected you to drive—let me think—a sixties Maserati 3500 coupe, or an Iso Grifo, Bentley S1, or perhaps a Facel Vega II?"

"All lovely cars but I'd actually bought the BMW for my dad's 75th birthday way back then. He'd never bought himself a nice car, boat, or even vacation. Everything he did was for his kids. He was an amazingly giving guy. We took it on a long drive all the way down the Coast Highway to LA, and then to San Diego and into Tijuana. We'd never gone to a strip club, shot tequila, or stayed up all night partying together before. In fact we hadn't spent that much time together since I was ten.

"And I still think of him every time I fire her up."

"That sweet little Zagato came from BC—I bought it from the original owner who was moving and clearing out his garage. It was hidden in the back. After I helped him roll it out into the sunshine after 30 years we both just stared at it without saying a word. I was panicked he was going to change his mind. It is just so unadorned, and beautiful.

"I walked around admiring it a few times and then noticed on the second loop some discolouring on the hood."

"What was it?" Tanner asked.

"Go have a look yourself Tanner and tell me what you see."

"Are those eyes? Yes, eyes with eyebrows."

"Take a step further back," Mr. Brant said.

"Ahhh, the eyes are those male and female symbols—the one with the plus sign for the woman and the hard-on for the man."

"Well, I've never actually thought of it that way but yes, you're right. Thank you for that.

"Anything else?" Mr. Brant asked.

"Well, let's see. Ah yes, there's lettering all down this side of the hood:

"F.
R.
O.
M.
Space
H.
E.
R.
E.
Space
T.
O.
Space

"Eternity! From Here to Eternity!"

"Not quite. Try again. And then figure out what its last duty was before being put away for almost forever."

"M.
A.

"Maternity! From Here to Maternity!

"I get it, it was a wedding car; and someone sprayed these words on it and never cleaned them off!"

"Well done, Tanner. And see the big faded heart on the front of the hood?"

"This is awesome Mr. Brant!"

"It sure is. The groom's best-man wrote it in shaving cream and then the newlyweds went off to Italy on a three-week honeymoon. When they returned it was permanently stained. But she loved it, so it was just left and never repainted."

"Glad you didn't try to buff it back to original, or repaint, but I know you're the original 'preservation class guy'."

"Yes sir. And check out what I found in it: Those eggcup

bells hanging from the rear view mirror, and a garter-belt between the front seats," Mr. Brant said with a smile.

"I bet you picked up a few garter-wearing birds in that Morgan Plus 8."

"Not precisely, you vulgar lout, but I did court my wife Keira in it."

"Well, I do feel somewhat embarrassed now but I'm sure to get over it: Over it!"

"I've just always liked the car, and the fact the company has stayed alive all this time. I had a 3-wheel Morgan years ago: now that was a blast. I bought this one down in San Carlos, California from some high-tech Kiwi. He'd sent them custom wood they used in the frame. Lift up that panel in the back and what do you see?"

"Is that a cricket bat?"

"Yup. It was his grandfather's."

"And a... hockey stick?"

"It was used by his favorite player who was someone named Orland Kurtenbach, or something like that. Why a Kiwi had a Canuck's hockey stick I'll never know."

"And a baseball bat?"

"You got the trifecta Mr. Hamilton, congratulations."

"You have the coolest car collection I've ever seen, and I've seen a lot, Mr. Brant."

"Thanks Tanner. I really appreciate that. It isn't a collection I went out and sourced. They're just cars that have come my way. I bought a few at auctions but mostly came across them rather serendipitously over many years."

"Another DS, I see. Looks like the first generation. Does it have the ultra-cool early dashboard?"

"It certainly does. I found it in a garage in Citrus Heights, California, just outside of Sacramento. Its serial number is only 4086. Over 1.3 million DS's followed it out of Quai de Javel in Paris. Only a handful of genuine first year DS's remain as they hadn't quite figured out the hydraulics, and the cars were magnets for rust.

"This one was from San Francisco's dealer *Executive Motor*s. One of the first D's in America but started its life on the wintery wet docks of New York City, as Paris HQ hadn't had the foresight to set up a dealer network *before* the cars arrived. They just sat in an open-air warehouse. Six months later — when Citroën executives had *finally* gotten around to setting up a sort-of dealership network — they went to retrieve the cars and were shocked to find what looked like 180 old, rusty cars. The DS's were trucked to a dry facility where their drivetrains were removed, engine compartments cleaned up and painted medium blue, and hydraulic lines painted gold to cover up surface rust. New bumpers were installed and some of the problematic hydraulic seals were replaced. As far as I can tell they were then sold as new. Or maybe as demonstrators.

"This one was parked in a garage in 1960 after a trip across the Mojave Desert by the original family. Seems they'd had some sort of breakdown, and the missus wasn't too keen with its unreliability so he stuffed it in the back of their garage and bought a new, less complex, ID version to replace it. 4086 never saw the light of day again."

"So it was only four years old when turfed aside?"

"'Turfed aside'? Another Canadianism?" Mr. Brant asked.

"Really? Maybe this is why so many people down here look at me funny when I talk."

"I could certainly support that hypothesis.

"It had just over 50,000 miles when we found it so it did get used a bunch over those first few years. But yes, it's very much like it was the day it was interned. After the father passed away, it was headed to the crusher until an Alfa guy saw it and thought it might be interesting to a Citroën person given how low the serial number was. I snatched it up the moment I heard — seems that everyone else in the Citroën community was scared as it was a brake fluid car that had sat for fifty years. They were probably pretty smart. But I did enjoy getting all dirty wrenching again. Most complicated car project I've ever attempted."

"You restored it yourself?"

"Not restored young Tanner. Resurrected."

"Oh yeah, the whole preservation-thing."

"Yes. Anyway, I tackled it myself but seriously leaned on my good friend Willy who's a walking Citroën encyclopedia. He sent me thousands of emails outlining exactly what to do when I got stuck. And I was always stuck. I'd send him the hydraulic components which he'd rebuild with LHM seals."

"LHM? I heard you mention something about LHM with the Chapron."

"That's the fluid Citroën used later in the DS's lifespan—mineral-based, not vegetable like the original LHS and LHS2 fluids. In America here we just used DOT 3 brake fluid. After sitting for fifty years the brake fluid had, in some pipes and recesses, turned to goo, and in others wreaked havoc as rust settled in. We had lots of conversations about whether to keep it original, or upgrade to LHM. We eventually decided to change it to LHM which added a lot of time and money but it's probably better in the long run. There are still days I wonder if we made the right call as this car is so original; but, if someone is even crazier than me they can always change it back to LHS. We didn't do anything irreversible."

"That's quite an accomplishment for someone as, how shall I say, 'elderly' as you are," Tanner joked.

"You see this cane here? It shoots poison darts," he said as he pointed it directly at Tanner's heart.

"When I was cleaning the DS out, when I first got it home, I found an old style Kodak film canister in the glovebox. I thought at first it was unused but then noticed it just hadn't been processed yet. I sent it off to my friend Gary in Vancouver who still has a darkroom and, sure enough there were a few photos of the family on it; and one with kids playing in a blow-up pool in the backyard. And, shockingly, you can see in the background that particular DS parked in their carport. I sent prints to the family and they appreciated it. Based on the age of the children they said it was taken in 1958 or '59. They then returned the favor and sent me an amazing photo of the car at a ranch somewhere with their young son Michael standing beside it, and another of it parked in the shade behind one of those old wooden billboards that cops always hid behind in old movies. It had 'Mojave Desert, August 1960' written on the back. It's one of my favorite photos of all time. I have it blown-up in the house, actually in my den, as Keira's not as impressed with it as I am for some strange reason."

"Women," Tanner said with an ersatz smile.

"I'd also mentioned to the family that really early DS's came with a little hand mirror tucked into a special recess in the glovebox and that they were always missing. Kim, a friend of mine, has been looking for one for at least a decade. A couple months later a package arrived in the mail with a few trinkets they'd found in the garage: the original yellow water reservoir for the squirters, tons of used parts which helped me figure out why it had been taken off the road—looks to have had some transmission problem—and their dad's detailed list of every gallon of gas that had ever gone into the tank, all repairs, and a plan on what needed to be done to get her roadworthy again. Also an extremely early workshop manual and parts book which looked like pre-production versions—printed in English thankfully, from Slough, England. His son Michael mentioned to me his dad had always planned to get it back on the road one day."

"What about the mirror?" Tanner said a bit sarcastically.

"Yes, quit confusing me, it was in the box too. Follow me, I'll show you."

"Oh yeah, that reminds me," Mr. Brant said as they shuffled over to the DS. "As I was going through the car before the flatbed arrived the mother came out with her walker to say goodbye to me—well, more likely the car—when she noticed a very torn old peach colored rag sitting in the trunk. She told me that particular towel had caused quite a stir way back then when her husband used it to fix the DS at her parent's ranch. She said it's funny how something can be so explosive at the time, but so insignificant later on in life—like Savannah biting your armrest. She shook my hand, said take care of Tortilla, and it was then I noticed a tear in her eye. She turned around and wheeled herself back into the house.

"That's been my favorite rag ever since."

"I love all those Corgi Toys. How many are there?"

"3,576. MIB."

"I know, I know, Mint-in-Box," Tanner jumped in, proving he too was a toy freak.

"The entire original collection from A to Z."

"Allard to Zil?" Tanner proposed.

"Well I don't know; and that's not really what I meant but let's go over and figure that out.

"The last one in was the ultra-rare #336 James Bond Toyota. You've heard of Adam Wilson, the once internet billionaire, right? He started collecting these somewhere in Eastern Washington, Pullman I think, as a little kid. It looks like he never took them out of the boxes. The ends aren't even a little bit worn or damaged. Personally, I like to play with them once in a while. Especially those Chipperfields circus trucks; but don't tell anyone now will ya?"

"Your secret is fairly safe with me Mr. Brant."

"Fairly?"

"I always like to have something embarrassing over my friends."

"Who said we're friends? You're a punk who drives a Honda van."

"Yes, but it has 17 cup holders, remember?"

"If you add up all the cup holders in this entire garage do you know how many you'd get?"

"Let me guess, zero except for that Signature coloured car over there?"

"Smartass. Yes. Coffee consumption is for cafes and breakfast nooks, not cars. Next thing you know they'll be adding microwave ovens to heat up breakfast sandwiches while you're suppose to be watching the road."

"Makes more sense than a glove compartment. Who wears gloves anyway? And if you do, no one stores them in there anyway. I vote for your brilliant mobile microwave compartment idea."

"Humbug. Back to cars please."

Gregory Long

"And a McLaren. An F1 McLaren. When did you get it?"

"Bought it brand new. Crazy money for a new car of course but after one drive you know it's very special. I read somewhere that Mr. Bean—I mean Rowan Atkinson—drives one as his daily driver. An F1 as a daily driver: Now that means he's both bloody wealthy and a true car guy: Good on him.

"Trailer-queens are on the other side of that coin: but it's too easy to point fingers at them as inferior; but—as objects of art—I want to take care of them too. A few of my preservation cars—the '56 DS, the Cobra, the 'Cuda in particular do pain me to drive on normal roads, with normal people milling about in normal Highlanders and Escapades. It's just that no matter how defensively I drive something can come out of nowhere and, in an instant, that last original first year DS is toast. So then you want them to go into museums, or be trailered around; and, well, you can't win. In the end I try to keep them all roadworthy and I'm a little more careful with some over others. And my little race track around the house does allow them to stretch their legs once in awhile."

"Thought you said you'd bought the Shelby Cobra over a new Stingray?"

"I did, in 1965. But this crazy thing was still available new in '68 as a left over '67. Everyone wanted the new Mako Shark Stingray in '68 so this wild one was still on the lot."

"It's a L88, then, I assume? Why wouldn't it be an L88—the rarest production, well semi-production, Corvette alive."

"I told you, they couldn't give it away. It takes 103 octane racing fuel to run properly. Can you imagine the same salesman trying to sell such a beast at your local Chevy dealer alongside a Biscayne wagon or Impala 4 door? God I loved those days."

"Isn't it rated at 430 horsepower but wasn't that bullcrap?"

"Yup, they say it actually pushed 560 brake horsepower at 6400 rpm. I never drove it much—too scary."

"Why do you, and those blokes on those British car TV shows, always say 'brake' horsepower and we just say horsepower?"

"I think brake horsepower refers to the horsepower that actually makes it to the wheels—where the brakes are. But, now that you mention it I'm not sure. And I think engines don't technically create horsepower they create torque. So, to answer your question more succinctly, I don't know."

"Incredibly cool car no matter what the true output," Tanner remarked as he checked the odometer.

"Damn. Only 3,761 miles."

"Mr. Brant."

"Call me Terence."

"Terence, nope, just can't do it, sorry, Terence. Nope, Mr. Brant... why are those three all parked over there—they all seem like 1973's?"

"Good eye. Yup all '73's.

"As I mentioned, I was an architect on a number of new ski hills and we'd got a contract to develop a big chunk of Whistler. It was a small town when we arrived. Had only one bank that was just in a converted trailer—and it was actually robbed once, and only once, because they stole the entire bank by just hitching it to a truck and driving off with it!

"I had put together a small group and we turned from being just architects to developers too. It was a scary time because the numbers were getting really big and we didn't know what we were doing; but, what the hell, we gave it a shot. We surprised ourselves by doing really well; and decided we all needed company cars to spend some of the profits. I'd just read a road-test comparison in *Car and Driver* of those cars so we decided to get a three-year lease on each one and trade them around with each other every six months. Can you name them, and I don't just mean make, but make, model, engine displacement or horsepower?"

Gregory Long

"Well, sure, the Grigio Ferro Metallizzato is obviously a Ferrari Dino 246 GTS 2.4 litre with 192 brake horsepower. Looks to have chairs and flares too. The Sable Métallisé one—I think its code is AC318—is a Citroën SM with swiveling headlights, and I suspect, the 170 horsepower 2.7 litre Maserati engine not the 3.0 as it looks to be a Canadian 5 speed with side markers. And the chartreuse one is obviously a 911 RS 2.7 Lightweight with ducktail and script delete. So that's 210 horsepower; and arguably the finest 911 of all time."

"I think it is; and I just never liked the tail so had it replaced with a conventional lid. The original ducktail is over there on the wall. I have a few old wooden duck decoys I used to hunt with stored on it for fun.

"And how do you possibly know each of the color's names? That is beyond scary! And you're right on the money except that the SM has a 3 litre as it was an automatic converted to 5 speed, but I won't take points off for that."

"I've always wanted to be a colour-namer," Tanner said. "I know that's nuts but ever since Plum Crazy, Lemon Twist, Sassy Grass, and Vitamin C came out I just took a fancy to learning the colours of cars I love."

"Wow, Tanner, you are nuts, but you're really a walking encyclopedia, or should I say, a walking Wikipedia now?

"I ended up buying all three after their leases ran out. They're all actually amazing vehicles—so different. The Dino is just so beautiful and handles so well but it's had a lot of bodywork and paint over the years as blasting up to Whistler all the time did a real number on it.

"Amazing how old 911's were just 'old 911s' not so long ago. The RS took quite a bit of work to get in the country but I've put on serious mileage since: 180,000 miles and it's only on its second drivetrain rebuild. When they said they're bulletproof, they weren't joking.

"That said, I have a '67 911S Targa in the shop right now. I try to do my own work but sometimes I just send them out. The 'S' is great when it's running right—I finally upgraded to electronic ignition and it doesn't gobble up spark plugs on a rapid basis anymore; but she was burning a lot of oil recently.

"It's got a pretty interesting story too: I was standing around the back of a stadium with a friend who worked with a concert promoter, just waiting for a *Simon and Garfunkel* concert to start when who should pull up but Art Garfunkel himself driving what was then a brand new 911S Targa: First year for the S and first year for the Targa. After the shock wore off I told my buddy I was going to get a 911S just like it one day. A couple years later I'd finally tracked one down in LA. I go have a look and it's the in the same red, I mean *Polo Red*, with black interior. Then the guy mentions Art Garfunkel was the original owner. And this all transpired on my actual birthday. Sold, I said, even before negotiating the price.

"You like Targa's, Tanner?"

"You know I didn't forever but they really appeal to me now. And you have the soft rear window which is the one everyone wants. The coupe is still nicer looking but I think the Targa is so special now that it's the one I'd want. Not sure everyone would agree with me though. But you've had it for over 40 years too. Wow. Original paint?"

"Yes, lots of rock chips and a few little dings but pretty nice overall, especially for red. I was tempted a few times to repaint years ago but I'm so glad I didn't. Only thing I changed out was the original Fuchs — put on some wider ones — the original 165's were just too small for the power/ weight ratio of the 'S': It's got downright scary at over 110. I kept the originals, just in case. And the radio died. I still have it in a box though — I keep everything, always have."

"I've got a 911 too," Tanner piped in. "I don't think I mentioned that yet? It's certainly no early 911S or an RS but I have a somewhat lighter pocketbook than you. Anyway, after 40 years of reading *Road & Track* I wanted to see what all the fuss was about. I set out to determine what was the best one for me and my pocketbook. I learnt about the 964, 993, 996, 997, Turbos, C4's, short hood, Targas, etcetera versions of 911's; and quickly focused on rear drive convertibles with air-cooled engines. That lead me to the 993 which, I'm sure you know, is the last version before water-cooling and, arguably, the nicest front headlight treatment while retaining the classic 'look'."

"Agreed," said Mr. Brant.

"I quickly dismissed the early, early cars as too expensive; and — already having a few older cars — I just wanted something I could jump in and enjoy. The 993 ticked — as they say—all the boxes. So now it was time to hunker down and find a 'perfect' one. I'd decided I wanted a convertible version—I just love open top cars even though the coupes are cooler. My purchase criteria was pretty straightforward: As close to a 100% original car as possible. See, Mr. Brant, we're on the same page. It must have original paint, interior, engine—matching numbers. It could have some blemishes as I intended to actually drive it so no trailer queens. Also I wanted low mileage, full history, and manual transmission was a given—no Tiptronic. I also preferred an 'interesting' colour. Red, black, silver and white are nice enough but I wanted something special."

"Tall order. How'd you find it?"

"I was in no hurry so I just waited for her to come along. And she did. On Craigslist in St. Louis of all places. It's a '96 911 Carrera Cabriolet. I bought it with 31,000 miles, and it has just under 37,000 now. It has the rare special order—and exquisite, if I do say so myself—colour of Avertine Green which looks black at night, dark green or dark blue in the sun—very strange, very captivating. It's original leather interior is cashmere, and perfect.

"I had a PPI completed by a Porsche specialty shop and they basically found nothing but a top that didn't close each and every time, perfectly—from lack of use, they said. This was fixed and it's worked great ever since. In fact the owner of the shop said, 'If you don't buy it, I will. It's an original, well looked-after, perfect 993. And they've probably hit their low in terms of price and will be a strong investment given their air-cooled engines—which most purists/ collectors covet.' I snapped it up and had it trucked out here. I'd heard you either get a problem-child 911 that cost a fortune to own, or one that will run hundreds of thousands of miles with basically only maintenance. I put new Yokohama's on the back but that's it.

"The original woman owner ordered it as a special order and sold it once it was just too hard for her to get in and out of. This 911 was her last, in a long line of Porsches, and the '30 year member of the Porsche Club' sticker on the windshield supported that."

"Great analysis Tanner. And sounds like it was very well bought. Don't you just love the hunt?"

"Sure do, but I interrupted you. Tell me all about the SM."

"The SM is magnificent; and the most misunderstood, mis-maligned car I have. We got it in the summer of '73 so it came with the US headlights and was an automatic: the worst spec. One of my partners really wanted an automatic; and I really wanted an SM, so we compromised. Once it came off lease I had the front-end converted to the proper European lighting. It was done in Vancouver at Parthenon Motors who had all the new parts as early Canadian SM's came with the proper glass-covered swiveling setup. The invoice for parts alone was a staggering $2,400 as I recall. And I dropped another $5,000 to have it converted to a 5 speed but those were good decisions — I've put over 150,000 miles on her and the engine is only on its second rebuild.

"Once they'd figured out that the Borg Warner automatic was crap; that you had to adjust and change the timing chains often; and that it was mandatory to replace the sodium-filled valves or they broke off and fell into that lovely Maserati 90 degree V6, you finally had a reliable SM. Those fixes weren't figured out until much later — long after Citroën left the market the following year — so SM's have always been viewed as colicky orphans. People finally seem to be figuring them out now as values are rising after being flat for decades. The fact that it's still one of Jay Leno's favorite cars speaks volumes."

"Well I've got an SM story for you," Tanner said. "A terrible SM story mind you. I was staring out the window of a city bus in Bellingham visiting a friend of mine going to Western Washington when a stunning white SM appeared out of nowhere: I was mesmerized by its lines as it pulled up to a stop light. My automotive trance exploded when it was rammed from the rear by a huge American car. Glass flew everywhere. Thankfully the driver's door of the Citroën was just opening as the bus pulled away."

"Ugh, poor thing. I've always wondered what happened to the SM Burt Reynolds stole from his girlfriend — who, incidentally, incorrectly referred to it as a Maserati which, I assume, drove the Citroën PR people crazy! It would have been a brand new car they dumped in the river — wonder if it was ever fished out and dried off?

Gregory Long

"And, as you say, that Signature Red one has got to be the only new car I've bought in years. It's not parked in here usually because it's the car my wife likes to drive every day. And, yes, she likes its coffee cup holders. Keira's not much into the old cars and even has the audacity to tell me my garage smells of oil! What does she know, it needs to smell of oil.

"Anyway, when Tesla first came out with their electric Lotus I was impressed with the little thing but it was too hard for me to get in and out of. I loved the technology and thought—like almost everyone else—the company would be toast soon enough but I still wanted one. Surprisingly they survived and then the Model S appeared. I put my deposit down for one sight unseen the first day. I didn't think it looked as radical as it could have but I was intrigued by the technology, how the frame was made up of batteries, how it had tons of room—even a trunk and a frunk. And I loved the huge iPad-looking thing in the dashboard, great for these tired peepers.

"Have you driven one Tanner?"

"No, but they seem to win every award; and I've not spoken to an owner that isn't enthralled with it."

"Well, I'm one of those folks too. The only complaints I can think of—and they're not really complaints, rather suggestions—is that they could be more comfortable. Suspension and seats are a little hard for my liking. And there's lots of road noise which, I assume, is a result of having such a silent power-plant.

"But I kept reading about how the journalists were calling them so innovative. Sure they have amazing battery technology, and it's an impressive overall package, but most of the groundbreaking work was done years ago. Actually a century ago when many cars were electric. It just took 100 years for battery technology to catch up; and someone as entrepreneurial, visionary, and gutsy as Elon Musk to make it happen. But was it really so innovative?

"So I got in touch with a journalist I know from MotorTrend and pitched him on pitting the new Tesla against my first year Citroën DS over there. Usually they do a Camaro against and Mustang, Corvette against Viper, Ferrari against Lamborghini sort of thing. But this couldn't be a performance test; it had to be, 'Which car was the more innovative'? Jonny told me he gets proposals for stories all the time and most are obvious, or dull, or both but loved this one and would pitch it to the editors. Long story short, they ended up coming up here and shooting a video test for two days with both cars: Tesla supplied a new Model S, and I supplied the DS."

"Tell me more. I remember watching that video and forwarding it around to all my Tesla-loving and Citroën-hating friends."

"You have Citroën-hating friends?"

"OK, not Citroën-hating per se but they just don't get them."

"Screw 'em.

"So now back to my story you so rudely interrupted. It started when they all arrived here at 6:30 in the morning. It was below freezing but, miraculously, sunny. The DS takes a while to warm up so we sat in the garage and got her ready for the drive out to Duvall where I'd done some reconnaissance the weekend before. Gorgeous roads along the meandering Snoqualmie River with the snow-covered Cascades as a backdrop—can't be beat."

"You actually got them out of this garage?"

"Well, you're right, it wasn't easy and I had to forcibly eject Jonny from the Bowlus. Not really, I successfully coaxed him out with an American cheese omelet."

"An American cheese omelet?"

"I know, thought it was a bit strange too but what the talent wants the talent gets. Especially as I was trying to butter him up. I did the driving out to Duvall in the DS with Jonny and, when we got to our first stop, he couldn't wait to take the wheel. The crew covered the front passenger window with video cameras and lights and they let me hide in the back seat as the film—I mean hard-drive—started to roll—I mean spin—and Jonny gave on-the-fly impressions of the DS and reviewed its ground-breaking innovations. We did more driving with the DS either following, or being followed, by the Mazda SUV camera-car. I was a bit worried as it was extremely foggy but the team loved it—the fog gave them an interesting new 'look'. Jonny did his commentary in the Tesla as well and, as the fog lifted, it was time to do some 'driving shots'.

"Jonny didn't really want to relinquish the DS. He'd just spent a ton of time in the Teslas with their *Car of the Year* awards—which Tesla won hands down—but also because he just couldn't stop smiling. When one gets to constantly drive the world's greatest new cars, its nice to know the humble DS, especially one that was close to 60 years old, and with only 75 horsepower, still captivated a true aficionado.

"So you know who won, right? Do you agree?"

"Yes, Mr. Brant, I wholeheartedly agree."

"And speaking of Citroëns I see that wonderful 'tank-like' vehicle over there sports a double chevron emblem on its radiator and a giant 4 on the side; but it doesn't look to be military—at least the white paint doesn't look very war-like."

"You're right, it was number 4 of 5 Kégresse Half-tracks brought over to northwestern Canada for an expedition by a millionaire Frenchman by the name of Charles Bedaux. Charles was friends of Andre Citroën and wanted to have his journey written about in all the papers. But the terrain was so difficult, and the bugs so bad, they went mad even though he'd brought along the essentials: a French chef, caviar, fine champagne, and both his wife and mistress.

"Of the five half-tracks only this one remains. And it was found in the forties when the Alaska Highway was being built. The story goes that two slid off cliffs—not sure what happened to the poor souls riding in them. And one was sent down a river on a raft to be blown up by dynamite for a scene in the movie—except the dynamite didn't discharge so the Citroën just sailed off down river eventually driving, I mean floating, off some waterfall. The final two were abandoned in Halfway River, BC when the journey came to an abrupt end. Someone found them years later in deplorable condition but was able to make this one out of them. I love driving it around the paddocks out there."

"Awesome, Mr. Brant. I'm sure you've heard of

Zikmund and Hanzelka then?"

"Yes, I have the three volume set of their tours around Africa and Latin America in T87's in the late 40's—I think 1947 to 1950. I have the only set I've ever seen in English; all others are in Czech. Their story actually inspired a couple friends of mine to drive their Tatra T87's on what they called the 'Three Oceans Tour': Roll the front wheels into the Pacific, Atlantic and, the most difficult of all, the Arctic Ocean. Both cars had just come out of extensive, and expensive, restorations. It's so great they took them on such an ambitious tour—especially as the Dempster Highway is still gravel. They have an amazing photo of them in August in the Yukon in a blinding snowstorm. They both made it back. Very impressive guys. And cars."

"Neat. Have you ever read the book *Three Against the Wilderness*?"

"Nope, never heard of it."

"You'd love it. It's about a pioneering family in the wilds of BC back in the early 1930s. My brother Bob gave it to me for my birthday one year. A Brit, Eric Collier, immigrates to Canada as a young man and knows nothing about living off the land. He eventually ends up marrying a local woman and having a son, Veasy. When Veasy was just an infant they packed up all they had and moved into an abandoned log cabin in the Chilcotin region. They lived off the land and rarely went into the little town which was a five-day hike away—yes, 5 days, not hours. They lived there for 26 years—through unbelievable hardship: severe illness, chilling cold, and near starvation.

"They were the original naturalists though. Eric's wife had a very elderly native Indian grandmother. I think her name was LaLa—who asked them, on her deathbed—to bring the beavers back. Seems they'd disappeared when the white man appeared. Eric figured out how to bring the ecosystem back into balance and the beavers not only returned but prospered."

"You're right, I do love stories like that."

"So I was reading the book and came across a passage where he wrote of finally replacing the horses with a Jeep. But the photos in the book clearly show Land Rovers. I wondered about this so went and googled Veasy Collier and gave him a call."

"Just like that?"

"Yup, just like that, Mr. Brant."

"I couldn't believe when I got him on the phone right away and told him how thoroughly I had enjoyed his father's book and how fascinated I was with his life. I then asked him if he'd had people, like me, calling him out of the blue. He said he use to get a lot of school kids writing letters mostly because they'd be doing a report on the book for school and wanted to clarify something. I then asked him about the huge Jeep-Land Rover controversy. He took a few seconds before answering: "Never had that question before but I think dad first got an army surplus Jeep right after the war but soon-after replaced it with a Land Rover. He then told me he'd just had the last one his dad used—a '69 he thought—towed to the dump because its frame was finally too far-gone. I heard Veasy passed away just a few years ago."

"Great story Tanner, thanks for sharing. I'm going to download it to my Kindle tonight."

"And while we're still on BC and cars I've got one for you, Tanner."

"Go for it, Mr. Brant."

"It's about my mother. When she was a little girl she saw a *boat* coming down the *road*. She screamed and ran into her father's arms as the gasping, snorting, excruciatingly loud contraption came floating down the main road and moored in front of the hotel. They ran over—as did everyone in their little town of Armstrong."

"Armstrong, BC? So you're Canadian too?"

"Well I guess so, sort of. Born here in the States. And my mom moved to Point Roberts—a sliver of land cut off from BC by the 49th parallel border—in Washington State when she was young. But, yes, I guess, technically I'm Canadian. But I still won't put vinegar on my French fries.

"It ended up being the first car she, and most others in town, had ever seen. She thought it was a boat, I assume, because that was the only frame of reference she had that billowed smoke like that and moved. I did a little research and it may have been a Flanders 20 automobile, around 1911; but it may have been earlier too as Vancouver had a couple cars as early as 1904. And supposedly Vancouver had the world's first gas station too!"

"Great stuff!" Tanner replied.

"So it's pretty clear you love a ton of different vehicles but I'm assuming your favourite marque is Citroën, right? Two DS's, an SM, even a Kégresse Half-track. And somewhere around here is a 2CV, and a Traction I suppose?"

"I've had a number of 2CV's over the years. Bought the Charleston like your mom's back in the late eighties and bought one on eBay about a decade or so ago. There it was, a brand new 1965 with just 36 miles. Bill Harrah had bought it for his museum in Nevada from the Beverly Hills factory dealer and had it trucked to Reno as he was told it wouldn't make it up the hills—which was utter nonsense. Anyway, there it had sat for decades—I'd even seen it on display there years before. When it appeared on eBay, I couldn't believe it. I learned the fine art of sniping and got it! When we went to pick it up it was sitting between a gold DeLorean and Harrah's Jerrari."

"You mean Ferrari?" Mr. Brant."

"Nope, Jerrari. Bill built his own Range Rovers I guess. He had a Ferrari V12 crammed into a Jeep Wagoneer. A couple of them as I recall.

"Now back to the 2CV story. Why do you keep knocking me off course anyway?"

"Just bored I guess," Tanner joked.

"You can leave anytime you want, you know."

"Leave? Just so you know I have no plans on ever leaving this garage. This is heaven to me."

"What'll Paige think?"

"She'd send her condolences, and my toothbrush. I wouldn't leave even if you held a poison-dart cane to my heart, or a loaded Glock. Incidentally, a man like you must have had a shooting-brake once in his life."

"Actually I did, now that you mention it. An old guy

Gregory Long

had it, together with a rather eclectic collection of a few really old Bentley racers, an Avanti, a Curved-dash Oldsmobile, and a Stanley Steamer he'd bought, and drove, when he was well into his nineties. The shooting-brake was a two-door Allard station wagon. An Allard Safari if memory serves me correctly. It was a woody with a monolithic Cadillac engine. I remember selling it but don't remember to whom, or where it eventually went. I believe I read they'd only made a half dozen of them back in the early '50s. The chap had found it on a used car lot in Victoria. No one wanted it; it was too cumbersome to drive and had a voracious appetite for gasoline. Perfect for me though.

"Now where was I again? Quit getting me off topic!"

"You were giving me your secret family recipe for cardamom meringue pie."

"Yes, the Harrah's car. See, I'm tight as a drum. I remember I looked underneath and was disappointed to see so many new parts until I realized they weren't new, just perfect, unused, never dirty, original parts assembled in late 1964 as a 1965 model.

"The museum administrator handed me the keys—still on the original little ring that matched the photo in the '65 brochure—a bunch of paperwork including the original invoice that even had a note hand-written on it to replace a trim piece in the back bumper as it had been damaged in transit; owners manual; and a coupon for the 500 mile check-up it was obviously never eligible for.

"I asked why they'd put it up for sale in the first place. She said it didn't fit the museum's new theme of Automobiles and US culture, or something like that. With the exception of Richard Dreyfuss driving a blue one in *American Graffiti*, and Maxwell Smart changing into his wedding suit in a yellow one while being chased by KAOS, I think they had a point. Their loss, my gain."

"I've always thought a cool collection would be to find and buy all the cars Agent 86 drove in *Get Smart*. Can you name them, in order, Mr. Brant?"

"I too loved that show. I was doing a lot of work at ski resorts in California in those days. Got to meet a bunch of the celebrities back then. Sugar Bowl in Tahoe was popular with the Hollywood set, I guess because of its relation to Mr. Disney.

They even named the peak Mt. Disney. So, let's see... Maxwell Smart started with a '61 Ferrari 250 PF Spider."

"What? No way!" Tanner said surprisingly. "Everyone knows it was a Sunbeam Tiger."

"You're not as smart—pun intended—as you thought, huh? The 250 was used in the pilot episode. I was actually offered the exact car years ago and passed on it, bought a California instead. So, yes, after that it was the '65 Tiger but they also used a plain Alpine in some scenes—just changed the script to Tiger on the side. Needed room to add a machine gun under the hood which the V8's size wouldn't allow—something like that."

"Well... sounds like you do know what you're talking about. I'll be doing some fact-checking on the Ferrari, by the way. The Tiger was in Carnival Red," Tanner snuck in.

"Then a '67 VW Karmann Ghia convertible, in blue. Right Tanner?"

"Correct. Neptune Blue."

"And finally a Shelby Mustang GT350 convertible. In blue as well?"

"Wrongo Mr. Brant! That was the Chief's car—a GT500 in Medium Blue Metallic."

"GT500 KR?"

"Nope, no KR, it was an early '68," Tanner confirmed.

"And you know what KR stood for, right?"

"Child's play: King of the Road," Tanner responded brightly. "So what was his last car?"

"Hmmm, I know this...give me a minute, it's buried in the recesses of my memory bank... it takes a while for the retrieval mechanism to spin up... ah, there it is: an Opel GT."

"Wow, Mr. Brant, I didn't expect you to pull that out of your ass, I mean, out of thin air. Nicely done. And, as I'm sure you're aware, it was in Regal Gold Metallic."

"Where was I again with the *interesting* stories?" Mr. Brant said cynically but without malice.

"Harrah's 2CV."

"Oh yes... but it was such an amazingly original car I couldn't drive it. I was so worried it was going to get hit and that would be that. Last 100% original sixties 2CV left. My brother John stayed over once, got up early to grab a cappuccino in town and inadvertently almost doubled its mileage. I still remind him it was the most expensive cup of coffee he's ever had. And he happily reminds me that I, indirectly, paid for it.

"I took it to a big Concours d'Elegance one summer and felt bad as it wouldn't be fair as it wasn't restored but a 40 year old brand new car. I was pissed off when one of the judges told me it would never win a Concours d'Elegance because it was too ugly! And, adding salt to the wound, they gave a prize to an early Beetle... I never took any of my so-called elegant, or inelegant cars back there again.

"So after staring at it for almost ten years, I decided to sell it on at Retromobile in Paris. If it were going to do well surely it would be in France where they continue to be an icon even though they've been out of production for almost 25 years. Bidding was fast and furious, for about three minutes and — when all the excitement died down — it had gone well beyond the top estimate.

"The stranger thing is that I'd had an identical 2CV years before. I'd heard about it when I was over in Victoria visiting friends and we'd gone to the Chinese Village for dinner. In the lobby were photos of famous people and local celebrities; and I was flabbergasted to see a photo of the British actor Sebastian Cabot standing beside the prototypical grey 2CV in the restaurant's parking lot. I enquired, and the manager said Mr. Cabot had retired to Victoria from LA and had brought his little 2CV with him. In fact he'd driven it up all the way."

"Sebastian Cabot? Never heard of him."

"Mr. French on the TV show *Family Affair*? He played an English butler to a family without a mother living in Manhattan. Their front door had its handle smack dab in the middle which, as an architect, both intrigued and irritated me. Ring a bell?"

"A door bell? Sorry... bad joke. Sadly I don't remember the front door's handle's position but I do recall the butler having an amazing voice, right?"

"He certainly did. He was Bagheera in Disney's classic *The Jungle Book*. Intrigued, I made a few inquires and found out Mr. Cabot had passed away but his wife still lived in Deep Cove, on the outskirts of Victoria near the ferry terminal. So what does a car-crazy person do?"

"They go look for it, immediately," Tanner replied.

"Correct, young man. So I found the address and went on out. First thing I noticed was a small wooden garage with an early E-Type FHC wearing California black plates. I knew I was certainly in the right place. I knocked on the door but alas no one was home. In the back was another, larger garage. I didn't want to trespass, so just left a note.

"I never heard back and forgot all about it until someone in Victoria told me there was an ad in the Times Colonist for a *'64 Citroën 2CV 6,000 miles, owned by famous person'*. I called the number listed and found out someone else had scooped in ahead of me and bought it from the family; and was now reselling as they were moving back to Ireland. They also had a lovely light blue low mileage DS21 at the time. I remember they wanted top dollar for them both so I just sprung for the 2CV— should have bought the DS too. Anyway, the Cabot 2CV had its original 425cc engine with only 18 horsepower. I can't imagine Sebastian—who was of rather ample girth—for the life of me driving it the 1,500 plus miles from Los Angeles to Victoria, but he did: I found an envelope containing a little booklet where he listed all the fill-ups—first one was $1.49. Also receipts from the gas stations he stopped at; and a chit from Andersen's Pea Soup in Buellton, California for $3.12.

"Incidentally, I do like US versions of foreign cars. Usually they had to add some special lighting, pollution or, so-called safety device. Both of my identical 2CV's had teardrop turn-signals added by the factory-dealer in Beverly Hills; but when they had to remove the little European turn-signals from the C-pillars they were left with two holes to deal with. Luckily the *double chevrons* from a DS fit perfectly so they just bolted them in, facing forward though, like an arrow. No marketing person in his or her right mind would approve such a flagrant disregard for the sanctity of a well-regulated identify today. Back then it was *'whatever'*. A friend of mine's son Richard had a summer job doing this actual job back in the mid-60's; and he's the one who told me that story. Can you imagine any car company doing such a thing nowadays?" Mr. Brant asked rhetorically.

"I met another gentleman who also bought one of these Gris Rose 2CV's at the Wilshire Boulevard dealer back then too.

Gregory Long

He said he arrived and was told he could pick any one he wanted. There were about a dozen, all identical grey with plush red fabric upholstery. They were the fancy AZAM model so no hammock seats. I so loved the early days of the foreign invasion of all sorts of crazy cars. How they sold any Isettas, 2CV's, Goliaths, Messerschmitts, Lloyds in those days is beyond me. Cheap transportation, I guess. But in Quebec, Wisconsin, New Hampshire, or even New York, it boggles the mind.

"That particular 2CV was another one my wife got in the divorce. A friend of mine eventually got hold of her — the car, not the wife — and luckily it's still in beautiful low mileage condition. The 2CV is arguably the best overall classic car I have. It's certainly the most honest."

"What do you mean, honest." Tanner asked.

"It just goes. Never needs anything. Most of these cars you need to coax into starting, and running. They're all old so I get it — but that's how many of them were when they were new too — but in a 2CV you just turn the key and go. Period. No elaborate starting procedure; no warming up: No this, no that. You can just ignore it and it'll always behave. It has lots of room. A beautiful ride. It's fast, enough. Top rolls back. And it always makes me smile. And everyone around it smiles too. Nothing extraneous even though the Charleston paint job is a bit garish for my tastes — not really true to its humble roots. But Keira likes it. Granted, that's not the definition of honest but it's just so... trustworthy. Ok. Maybe honest, trustworthy, and a good friend.

"And, yes back to your original question, my overall favorite company would be Citroën. I've loved so many cars over my life though: brass era stuff, to Nomads and Woodies, Avanti's to Duesenbergs, and everything in-between from Toyota 2000GT's and FJ40's, to appreciating Fiats and Mercedes of all flavors. But it was Citroën that created — out of thin air — the Traction Avant, the 2CV, and the DS: All shockingly innovative cars that also went on to huge commercial success. Everyone could afford one — they brought true innovation to the masses.

"And I've always loved going to Citroën gatherings: you get the so-called hippy with a beat-up multi-colored 2CV parked next to the shimmering quarter million dollar DS convertible. And they both have a strong common bond, especially here in the States where the cars are so rare.

"Citroën took enormous risks—and had extremely long production runs—that meant all were well ahead of the curve. And that's why I appreciate them so. They combined so much thoughtful innovation into an overall compelling package ahead of everyone else. I was reading *Steve Jobs* and he seemed to follow a similar philosophy: Don't necessarily listen to your customers to determine what they want, leapfrog what's currently out there, sweat every single detail, and make it as pure as possible. The 2CV embodies this sentiment the most. But each of the milestone Citroëns were bristling with new, and in most cases, better."

"Oh, I see over there you do actually have a Traction as well. A Citroën aficionado certainly needs a Traction and you, of course, have the rarest of the rare, an 11 Convertible. Wasn't Mrs. Michelin given one when they took over Citroën after the launch of the Traction when Citroën went bankrupt and Andre Citroën died?"

"That's the story I heard too but that was a 15CV. I've also heard it's all not true so, overall, who knows? Go have a look at the front of the Traction, you might be in for a bit of a surprise."

"Nicely done, Mr. Brant. I read about this in a car mag awhile back where someone made a faux V8 22CV and faked everyone out at a big Citroën meet—the ICCCR, I think it's called—until he came clean a little while later. It was an amazing forgery I read."

Mr. Brant smiled and said nothing.

"You got that car, cool."

Mr. Brant continued to smile and say nothing.

"You've got to be joshing me. No f'ing way."

"Can't confirm or deny Mr. Hamilton, on the grounds it may incriminate me."

"You're pleading the fifth?"

"Guess so."

Gregory Long

Tanner poured over every millimeter of the non-fake 22CV Traction.

"I'm speechless. You actually have the real one. How the heck did you get it? This must have an incredible story."

"It does; and, of course, I can't say. I usually don't keep it up here but I took it out yesterday."

"'*Up*' here? So there's a '*down*' there too?"

"Ummm, no?" Mr. Brant said sheepishly.

"You don't sound very convincing."

"This could be a huge mistake. I'm assuming that if I ask you whether you can be trusted you'll say yes but it won't really mean much..."

"What have you got down there? Jimmy Hoffa's body?"

"No, nothing illegal, I've just enjoyed a lack of publicity. I don't like people prying. I don't like being made a fuss of. That's why I kept pushing you to be our Tatra-gate spokesperson.

"And I've always disliked how people of means can be perceived as so important if they just buy a certain rare car. The ads in the classic car magazines say something like, 'You'll be welcomed to all the best vintage events if you bring this car'. Talk about buying your friends. The buyer didn't need to do anything but sign a check, or less—just have the money wired by his financier. Then they wear one of those Panama hats, a blue blazer, and puff-up their chests—they don't even know a damn thing about the car they've brought, or even how to correctly spell Ferrari or Porsche."

"Still haven't got over them calling your 2CV inelegant I see," Tanner replied.

"That, and how having old cars has turned into such a big business, with the elite auctions, $275 event tickets, and so much big hair."

"Yes, big hair and big air, but the majority of the money is raised for charity," Tanner chimed in.

"And then there's the guys who can't stop themselves from putting Ferrari insignias on their Dinos. And the SM people who feel obliged to add a Maserati label somewhere. And those Intermeccanica Convertible D replicas that are really impressive cars in their own right but people are just compelled to add Porsche logos."

"Speaking of car logos, which ones do you like, Mr. Brant."

"BMW is really beautiful: simple, traditional, perfect actually. And I like Citroën's Double Chevrons as it directly connects to their history of innovation—in this case with their inventive helical gears that all cars use today. I like MG, Rolls-Royce—especially the early 'red letter' Rolls-Royces which signified the passing of Rolls, or Royce, can't remember which one."

"Not true. Another common misconception Mr. Brant. It's because the red letters clashed with some of the new more vibrant colours people were choosing in the early thirties."

"Nonsense."

"Bet, Mr. Brant? You put Ferrari badges on your Dino if you lose."

"And you jump in the pond, fully clothed, if I win."

"Damn, you're not really going to make me put them on, right? I'd rather jump in the pond."

"OK, I'll let you off this time but see, you can teach old dogs new tricks, Mr. Brant."

"Correct. Eighty-seven does catch up on you."

"You sure have a lot of hair. Or is it a well-crafted toupee?" Tanner said with a smirk.

"A barber told me when I was 13 I'd be bald as a cue ball by 21. It really bothered me but he was obviously just pulling my leg, or just plain wrong."

"And do you wear coloured contacts?"

"Are you partially brain-dead?"

"Yes, but that's not important right now. Your eyes are so blue they look almost artificial."

"Why thank you, I think."

"Ha, just pulling your leg, just like that barber. But you do, in fact, have lovely eyes."

"Well, it still amazes me I'm this old and still driving. Still going *fairly* strong."

"*Very* strong if you ask me. And, well, what about that whole basement thing?"

"Thought you'd forgotten."

"Not a chance."

Mr. Brant walked over to the wall of Corgi Toys, flipped a concealed switch in the shelf, and the wall slid across. "Told you I was a Bond fan."

There were only a few cars, and one open space for the Traction. Each of the cars were covered except for the one in a glass box.

"Care to guess?"

"Love to. First one here is a Mustang Fastback. I can just tell. And if there's a Mustang hidden away it's surely the '68 driven by our friend Lieutenant Frank Bullitt."

"Have a look."

Sure enough the Highland Green paint shone like new. Everything was there. Everything clones or tribute cars had tried to replicate over all these years, but this was the real thing. The Holy Grail of the movie car world: Steve McQueen's '68 Mustang GT 390 Fastback. The one that's been missing for 40 plus years.

"Bought it from the third owner. The second owner sold it to buy a Vega station wagon for his wife. Wonder if they're still married? Anyway, I bought it from a guy back east. Deal was that he'd always say he has it stored away and didn't want anyone to see it. I told him I'd give him an extra $5,000 if he kept quiet until I either died or sold it. He smartly said, 'With 5% interest per year'? I agreed. That's serious cash today. He called me the other day to check in our deal; and I confirmed it, again."

"I guess I could open the curtains up for a bit of light," Mr. Brant said as he pulled a cord on the right side of the wall. Lights automatically illuminated and another large scrunched-up piece of metal appeared.

"Go have a look and tell me if you can figure it out."

Tanner walked over, did a quick survey and blurted out, "No way!"

"You won't tell anyone, right?"

"How the hell did you get this? Are you sure it's real? It can't be real. It sure looks real!"

"It's real."

"It's the actual clip of 550-0055, really?" Tanner said skeptically.

"You can read that black script as well as I. In fact, probably better than me now. And notice the remnants of red paint across the fender tops?"

"So, how did you possibly get it? It disappeared in 1960."

"Barris sold it to me for a grand under the proviso I tell no one. But the statute of limitations has certainly run out after fifty plus years so I'm telling you. I'd still like to sort of honor my commitment to George so mum's the word, OK?"

"Yes, of course, but wow. I'm in the presence of the *Little Bastard* himself. This is like a religious experience."

"Better," Mr. Brant said with a smile.

"It's time to see what's in the glass box over there. Looks like an early Corvette. Clearly there's a story there," Tanner said as they walked over. "It gives off a bit of a *Silence of the Lambs* vibe though."

"Really? A caged Vette is akin to a psychopathic mass murderer?"

"It's eerie: Story please."

"I bought it from a guy who'd just bought a convenience store down in Eugene that had this car—in this box—in the middle of it. He wanted to remove it as he deemed the floor space too valuable. Supposedly he'd told the old guy he'd definitely keep it in the store, and within the box, but the moment the paperwork was signed he put in a classified ad and I snapped it up. He didn't really care whether it was a real '53 or not. Couldn't tell a '53 from an '83, I bet. Anyway, he was going to throw out the box but of course I thought that was the most interesting part. Customers—over all those decades—had come in and stuck those old stickers you use to collect of places you traveled to for your rear window — you know, like Yosemite, or Yellowstone. I've always loved those window stickers — they're folk art to me — so now I have a grand collection of those too!"

Tanner's eyes were then diverted to a chopper on the other side of the room.

"And of course you have Peter Fonda's Harley Captain America from *Easy Rider*. And the most iconic helmet in the entire world. You know I'm going to fall over very soon. I just don't know what you could possibly have under that final cover except Mr. Bond's stolen Aston Martin DB5."

"It wasn't stolen," Mr. Brant said in a hushed tone. "That was a grand diversion. As I said, I don't like people bothering me so I did a deal with the owner in Florida and we just faked the whole stolen thing. I personally took my enclosed car trailer down there, drove DP216/1 on, and quickly brought it up here. It's the actual 'effects' car so has all those cool gizmos from Q still on it. Have a look, take off the cover. Ejector seat doesn't work; I tried it with wife number two. Now you see why I have such a long windy driveway? Only way to give a few of these a good workout."

"Didn't the insurance company pay out $4 million or something on it?"

"Yes, and no. They said they'd paid it out but never did. I just gave them the business to insure my fleet here, and a lot of buildings, and they said, 'fine'. It's nice to work with a small family company sometimes."

"Who keeps them all going?"

"Me, I love to wrench but my back is getting pretty bad. Perhaps there's someone around here named Tanner I could trust to keep his mouth shut and help me tinker with them?"

"I do know of such a character but he doesn't come cheap: he demands to be compensated with mounds of Mr. Tasty's corn beef hash... I feel like a five year old but... can I just sit in them?"

"Of course, son. Breathe in that Connolly leather and Wilton carpets; and the GT's vinyl and plastic. Both intoxicating, each in their own way.

"Then do you want to check out my Reading Room?"

"Do bears shit in the woods?"

"I assume so; and I despise people who find that idiom funny."

"I'm not sure it's technically an idiom." Tanner replied quickly.

"Of course it's an idiom."

"Is 'It's raining cats and dogs' an idiom?" Tanner queried.

"Yes."

"Is 'She's pulling your leg' an idiom?"

"Yes."

"Is 'The early bird catches the worm'?"

"Yes."

"Ha, no! It's a proverb. Just like 'Does a bear shit in the woods?'" Tanner said energetically.

"A proverb is an idiomatic phrase," Mr. Brant said.

"But, is an idiomatic phrase an idiom?"

"Yes."

"I don't believe so."

"Well, you're the newspaper editor."

"Online editor."

"OK, so where were we?"

"I was taking you up on your offer of going to the Reading Room," Tanner replied.

"OK. And to answer your question, yes I believe bears must defecate in the woods given they actually live only in woods."

"Mr. Brant, I'd prefer you didn't use such lowbrow idiomatic phrases in my presence."

"Follow me, defecate-head."

"Where are we going? Tanner asked.

"Crazy, want to come?" Mr. Brant responded quickly, just like he'd said it a thousand times before…

Table of Cars:

1st Gear: Breakfast
- 1970 BMW 2800 CS Coupe
- 1967 Saab Sonett II

2nd Gear: Lives of Interesting Cars:
1 – 1957 Ferrari 250 Testa Rossa Scaglietti Spyder
2 – 1967 Citroën DS 21 Chapron Décapotable
3 – 1967 Jaguar XK-E Fixed Head Coupe
4 – 1974 Land Rover Series III
5 – 1957 Mercedes Benz 300SL Roadster
6 – 1971 Plymouth Barracuda Convertible
7 – 1950 Tatra Tatraplan T600

3rd Gear: It's a Beautiful Day for a Tatra Hunt
- 1967 BMC Mini Moke
- 1967 Panhard 24BT
- 1968 Buick Wildcat
- 1972 Citroën 2CV
- 2001 Saab 9-3 Viggen

4th Gear: More Lives of Interesting Cars:
8 – 1934 Citroën 22CV Convertible
9 – 1957 Maserati 200Si
10 – 1935 Bowlus Road Chief, Front Kitchen
11 – 1994 Morgan Plus 8
12 – 1956 Citroën DS19
13 – 1957 Jaguar XKSS and 1957 Jaguar D-Type

5th Gear: Lunch
- 2002 Chevrolet Silverado 1500 Regular Cab
- 1953 Jaguar XK120 Drop Head Coupe

6th Gear: Even More Lives of Interesting Cars:
14 – 1961 Alfa Romeo Giulietta Sprint Zagato
15 – 1967 Toyota 2000GT
16 – 1935 Tatra T77a
17 – 1956 Volkswagen Beetle
18 – 1948 Tucker Torpedo

Found / FoundCarsOfCascadia.com

19 – 1935 Quinte
20 – 1953 Chevrolet Corvette

Overdrive: The Garages of Mr. Brant

1 - The Roundhouse
- 1965 Shelby Cobra 289
- 1965 Amphicar 770
- 1994 McLaren F1
- 1967 Chevrolet Corvette L88 Coupe
- 1973 Ferrari Dino 246 GTS
- 1973 Citroën SM
- 1973 Porsche RS 2.7 Lightweight
- 1967 Porsche 911S Targa
- 1993 Porsche 911 Convertible
- 2013 Tesla Model S
- 1934 Citroën Kégresse Half-Track (*Quinte*)
- 1964 Citroën 2CV AZAM
- 1965 Citroën 2CV AZAM
- 1968 Ford Mustang GT 390 Fastback
- 1964 Aston Martin DB5

2 - The Crow's Nest

3 - Brantville

2. The Crow's Nest

They sauntered to the side of the garage and slowly up a set of winding stairs to another room that sat directly above. One entire 180-degree side was covered with slightly curved windowpanes facing southwest across the grounds. One could see the driveway cum racetrack circling the house with the pond down and to the right; and what looked to Tanner like a runway.

"I've sure got a lot of questions as I look out there but first one is, 'Is that an airport?'"

"Sort of. Don't get any use out of it any longer — a few of my friends use it once in awhile though. That Quonset hut down there has my '53 Piper Cub in it. I haven't flown in it for years now; but can't for the life of me come to sell it either. I've got skis and floats for it too; and taken it all over Washington State, BC and the Yukon. Even flew all the way to the Northwest Territories to hunt bighorn sheep one summer. Boy, now that was an adventure. As they say, 'Time to spare? Go by air.'"

"What?"

"With an old plane like that you're at the mercy of the weather; and of gracious people who live on lakes should you be grounded by rough skies."

"Isn't a Piper Cub pretty small to fly all over the North?"

"Yup, just a tandem two seater but I love it—I've had fancier planes but I always come back to the Cub. Similar, I guess, to having all these old, relatively slow cars—there's just something about them it's difficult to put your finger on. Too bad you don't fly."

"How do you know I'm not a pilot?" Tanner asked, somewhat taken aback.

"You called it an airport, not an airstrip. It's clearly an airstrip given it's on grass. I'll get one of my buddies to take you up some day soon; maybe go fly-fishing at a little place we have up in the Cascades. It's just a shack on an unbelievably beautiful lake. We call it Secret Lake. Cabin's pretty sparse: stocked with some canned food, a couple of bunks, a wood stove for heat, two chairs made of branches and antlers; and an amazing river running through it: The lake, not the cabin. Too tough for me to get there now but Bob's a great guy—he'll take care of you. We've only ever taken a select few folks up there over the years but I reckon you'll cut the muster. But no—how do you say—social media updates, my friend."

"You can trust me Mr. Brant."

"I know… follow me into the library, Tanner," Mr. Brant said, as he opened the door. "It's humidity controlled to keep everything as pristine as possible."

In front of Tanner were rows and rows of file cabinets. All exactly the same, and perfectly aligned. The walls were floor-to-ceiling bookshelves, complete with a cool sliding ladder, containing hundreds, if not thousands of magazines and books.

"This is my reference library for everything cars and

motorcycles. The file cabinets are full of brochures going all the way back to the late 1800's. I stopped collecting in 1974 when I just lost interest in new stuff. And when eBay arrived I was able to fill in a few I'd been looking for forever but half the fun was gone. The minute you can just go online, look up something, pay the asking price with your Visa, and have it just appear in the mailbox, the hunt is over, prematurely. I use to go to Retromobile, and little shops all over France, Germany, Sweden, Czechoslovakia, California, Japan, looking for interesting pieces. Care to try to stump my collection? Name a car and see if I have it."

"A Deutsch Bonnet. In French?"

"Sure, but too easy."

"OK, a US brochure."

Mr. Brant walked over to the penultimate cabinet on the left side stacks and pulled out an old 1959 brochure that was on its last legs.

"Wow, and in English," Tanner exclaimed.

"Yes, and check out the letter that came with the brochure. I challenge you to find any other written material on a Canadian DB."

Tanner took the one page letter from:

Auto-France Ltée,
Exclusive Distributors Citroën and Dyna Panhard,
7144 Cote des Neiges Road,
Montreal,

January 14, 1960

Mr. Ernie Brickle in Kindersley, Saskatchewan,

... and read it out loud:

Dear Sir:
As we are the Canadian Distributors of the Deutsch Bonnet, your letter to Vendome Motors Corporation of New York has been forwarded to us for attention. We have been selling the "Super Rallye" and "Sports Coupe" but do not expect to receive additional cars until early summer time. We have at present one "Super Rallye", orange

colour, which is being featured in a local sports car exhibition. This will last ten days. This car sells normally for $4,700. If you are interested, we can offer you this car at a substantial reduction due to it being used for exhibition purposes. New car guarantee will apply, of course.

We enclose copy of a brochure of the "Sports Coupe" showing specifications. We also enclose a brochure of a "Rallye Luxe" which is in French.

Yours truly, B. Johnson

"Isn't that amazing?" Mr. Brant questioned. "Nice they offered a discount as it was being used for exhibition purposes. I bet it was more like a substantial reduction because it was January in Montreal! And I bet they didn't move too many even in race season. They were great cars though. Those two cylinder engines powered a lot of successful wins back then including class wins at Le Mans, Sebring, and the Mille Miglia.

"Try again."

"OK, how about a brochure for the DB Cooper Tatraplan?"

Mr. Brant pulled out a large, multi-page brochure with an illustrated bright red Tatraplan on the cover drawn in the shadow an aircraft.

"Here you go. And look, it even says Shorters Electric, Victoria BC on the back."

"Amazing. Imagine if this was the brochure for the Cooper car?"

"It might just be. There's a name and address penciled here on the back:

Scott Chapman
3 something 63 Oak Bay Road
Victoria BC
MUrray Hill 5-997 something

"I think we just found our next adventure Mr. Brant."

"Sounds good to me but it was bought only 60 years ago so it'll be akin to a needle in a haystack."

"Idiom, or idiomatic phrase, Mr. Brant?"

Gregory Long

"Tanner, you don't have many friends do you?"

"How'd ya know, Mr. Brant," Tanner said with a smile. "So what do you have in here? Seems to be much more than pamphlets and brochures."

"I have full sets of *The Motor, CAR, Car and Driver, Road & Track, MotorTrend, Hemmings, Automobile, Automobile Quarterly* and most of the British car mags like *Classic & Sports Car and Classic Car Magazine*; and the newer ones like *Top Gear* and *Octane*. Full set of *Sports Car Market* and the earlier *Alfa Market Letters* Keith started out with; a bunch of French magazines; and of course Holland's *CitroExpert*. And, over there, are the books. For many years I just couldn't stop myself from buying nice car books. There are probably books about most cars you're interested in. Feel free to come over and do research anytime but make sure you wear those white gloves when looking at the old pieces."

"Thanks so much. You know I'll be taking you up on that. So here's a dumb question: what's your favourite book or brochure here?"

"Actually that's easy. It's my AutoBiography. See those big leather bound books over there? I spent a ton of time going through all my old pictures and all the information I had on all the cars I've owned. Have a flip through. Keira is into *Creative Memories* and was busy working away on creating all these great books of old photos, mementos, and stories; and compiling them into really nice books. A photo album is such a waste as it's the stories that give the context to the photos that's so important. She was doing such an incredible job of them, I decided to join in. It was lots of organizing, cutting, designing page layouts and, surprisingly I found it extremely relaxing and fulfilling. It allowed me to remember lots of great cars; and wonderful adventures with friends I wouldn't have recalled unless I'd had the trigger of pulling these books all together. I call them my AutoBiographies, get it? All those little yellow rectangles, with the car's make, model and year denote something I actually owned. You should start your own book."

"I think I'll do just that, even if it'll be just one pretty thin volume to start."

Found / FoundCarsOfCascadia.com

Table of Cars:

1st Gear: Breakfast
- 1970 BMW 2800 CS Coupe
- 1967 Saab Sonett II

2nd Gear: Lives of Interesting Cars:
1 – 1957 Ferrari 250 Testa Rossa Scaglietti Spyder
2 – 1967 Citroën DS 21 Chapron Décapotable
3 – 1967 Jaguar XK-E Fixed Head Coupe
4 – 1974 Land Rover Series III
5 – 1957 Mercedes Benz 300SL Roadster
6 – 1971 Plymouth Barracuda Convertible
7 – 1950 Tatra Tatraplan T600

3rd Gear: It's a Beautiful Day for a Tatra Hunt
- 1967 BMC Mini Moke
- 1967 Panhard 24BT
- 1968 Buick Wildcat
- 1972 Citroën 2CV
- 2001 Saab 9-3 Viggen

4th Gear: More Lives of Interesting Cars:
8 – 1934 Citroën 22CV Convertible
9 – 1957 Maserati 200Si
10 – 1935 Bowlus Road Chief, Front Kitchen
11 – 1994 Morgan Plus 8
12 – 1956 Citroën DS19
13 – 1957 Jaguar XKSS and 1957 Jaguar D-Type

5th Gear: Lunch
- 2002 Chevrolet Silverado 1500 Regular Cab
- 1953 Jaguar XK120 Drop Head Coupe

6th Gear: Even More Lives of Interesting Cars:
14 – 1961 Alfa Romeo Giulietta Sprint Zagato
15 – 1967 Toyota 2000GT
16 – 1935 Tatra T77a
17 – 1956 Volkswagen Beetle
18 – 1948 Tucker Torpedo

Gregory Long

19 – 1935 Quinte
20 – 1953 Chevrolet Corvette

Overdrive: The Garages of Mr. Brant

1 - The Roundhouse
- 1965 Shelby Cobra 289
- 1965 Amphicar 770
- 1994 McLaren F1
- 1967 Chevrolet Corvette L88 Coupe
- 1973 Ferrari Dino 246 GTS
- 1973 Citroën SM
- 1973 Porsche RS 2.7 Lightweight
- 1967 Porsche 911S Targa
- 1993 Porsche 911 Convertible
- 2013 Tesla Model S
- 1934 Citroën Kégresse Half-Track (Quinte)
- 1964 Citroën 2CV AZAM
- 1965 Citroën 2CV AZAM
- 1968 Ford Mustang GT 390 Fastback
- 1964 Aston Martin DB5

2 - The Crow's Nest
- 1956 Deutsch Bonnet Super Rallye

3 - Brantville

Found / FoundCarsOfCascadia.com

3. Brantville

What are those old buildings down there by the dock?"

"Want to go for a walk? My doctors say I should keep moving."

"All these cars and you wanna walk? How's that senility-thing treating ya?"

"You know, no one talks to me the way you do. You're quite disrespectful. And funny as hell. Keep it up. Now, get off your fat ass and I'll race you down to the pond. Last one in's a rotten egg."

"Really?"

"Yes, Tanner, you run down, hurl yourself in—fully

clothed preferably — and I'll be right behind you. Trust me. I have no problem being a rotten egg."

"Speaking of swimming in ponds, lakes, or any body of water for that matter, don't you cringe, Mr. Brant, when you always hear this dialogue:

'How's the water?'
'It's OK, once you get in.'

"Why do we, as a human race, have to say these words, exactly the same, each and every time? Everybody already knows the answer but has to ask. The boldest person has clearly gone in first, and always says 'It's OK, once you get in' mostly because they want you to share in their misery. And everyone already knows this. And everyone knows that unless you're doing a polar bear swim that it will, in reality, be 'OK once you get in.' Doesn't that just drive you nuts Mr. Brant?"

"No."

"Well, hopefully now that I've brought it to your attention you'll be as irked as I."

"Probably not. But what does bother me is these wildly overused phrases, *'It's only original once'*. And, *'It's worth what someone's willing to pay for it'*. Now those phrases drive me bonkers. Again, everyone says them like they're providing some insightful pithy comment for the first time: that it's a new brilliant thought they'd just come up with. Anytime someone says it to me now I just tune out and usually walk away. I know it's rude — and I know it shouldn't bother me so much — but I can't let it go."

"We both clearly need professional help Mr. Brant."

"And to answer your question of long ago, that's Brantville down there," Mr. Brant said as they strolled down the hill. "Some guys like to build their own western town, or a turn of the century type place with a blacksmith's shop, and a mock saloon with those swinging doors — or something like that — me, I wanted a little lake spot with a few old garages for boats and cars, and a small motor court for when my relatives visit.

"So, over years of self-inflicted aimless travel around England and the Continent I'd come across some pretty amazing spots I decided to replicate. One was an amazing garage where dust and cobwebs completely covered a couple of forever-parked Bugatti's. The cars were interesting but I was more taken with the shop itself. Really old rusted tools left out as if they'd just been used, amazing ancient cans of oil with Bugatti's logo on them, everything covered in thick dust. And at the end of the garage a huge beautifully crafted wooden tool bench with a vise the size of your head. With assorted wooden boxes strewn around, and under the bench.

"I kept in almost constant contact with the family who owned the house, garage, and cars and asked them to call me, day or night, if they ever wanted to sell any of it. Sadly, they rang me up after they'd made a deal on the cars and the house but said the garage was still full of junk and was I interested? I jumped on a plane late that same night to Brussels, rented a truck, and drove to Ronse. Thankfully it was exactly as I remembered. The cars were still there but would be retrieved soon — good thing I got there before them. I'd brought my Leica and snapped a ton of shots in both black and white, and color. They're in my AutoBiography books now.

"I then secured a great number of boxes and, like an archeologist, went about dissembling and secretly marking everything so I could reassemble it all properly back here."

"And that, I deduce, is what's in at least one of those buildings down there?" Tanner asked.

"Yes sir. But watch out for the grass over there, it's deceivingly moist — you can see where I drove the Kégresse through it when I was playing hobby farmer: Boy that was fun."

Down by the dock were three major out-buildings, and three identical cottages. Tanner peered in the dirty windows of the first building nearest to the pond.

"Fake dirty windows. Don't want anyone looking in. I've got a wonderful 30's Duke wooden boat in there from Port Carling."

"Muskoka, right?"

"Yes, between Rosseau and Mirror Lake; and it's clearly too big for the pond but I like to just leave it out, tied to the dock, in the summer. Looks peaceful. I use it to putter around with the little ones when they visit. Standing here reminds me of a dog we had years ago now, a plump, or should I say 'big-boned' rescue dog of many colors named Nike who loved to swim after tennis balls out there. Strange thing was, though, she'd always dive right off the dock, swim out and pick up the ball in her mouth but continue to swim clear across to the other side of the lake. She'd then get out and run all the way back. She never figured out she could have just done a 180 after nabbing the ball. She got a lot of extra exercise that way though, but somehow still kept hold of her extra blubber.

"And the kids love that little BRG punt over there too—they just float around on it all afternoon trying to catch fish, frogs, and the odd turtle."

"Why's the boat called the BoJoGeMo?"

"I have no idea. Came that way."

They then sauntered over to another building. It had two wooden doors that rolled straight out of the way, leaving space for three cars. Three Jaguars to be specific, covered in dust and spider webs.

"What do they call those things hobbyists make where they take toy cars and create a scene like they're in the pits at a racetrack in…"

"… or three classic Jaguars in a garage in Tottenham, or somewhere British-sounding like that?" Tanner interjected. "A diorama."

"Yes, that's it. So I decided to make my own, life-size though."

Tanner walked ever so carefully between the E and D and stood, in awe, at the workbench. It was exactly how Mr. Brant described it, filth and all.

"Isn't it grand? I love hanging out here. Can't really work on anything though because everything'll get too clean."

"I know these should be replicas but, knowing you like I do, they aren't. You have a real D-Type, an XKSS, and a FHC eType just sitting here for the explicit job of acquiring dust? Isn't that beyond crazy?"

"Yes, yes it is. But it was my dream to come across something like this so I just made it."

"Aren't you worried about mice, water damage, or juvenile delinquents?"

"It might look dirty and drafty but it's tighter than Fort Knox. The latest in HVAC—all hidden of course. And, as for delinquents—like you—it's got alarms up the wazoo; and rotating knives that neatly slice up anyone taller than five feet."

"Not true."

"Correct, too much Monty Python when I was younger."

"So, tell me all about these delicacies; I'm dying to know. And doesn't everyone already know where all the D-Type's and XKSS's are in the world? Kind of breaks your code of secrecy, doesn't it?"

"The D-Type's have a rather, how shall I say, *involved* history. Have you ever heard about a significant portion of the Jaguar factory burning down back in '57?"

"Yes, and only because it happened on my—and President Lincoln's—birthday: February 12th."

"Well that's *sort of* interesting. Anyway, of the 25 D-Types being converted into road-going XKSS's only 16 supposedly survived, leaving 9 perished."

"Supposedly?"

"Yes, this is the seventeenth XKSS. And that D-Type increases their count to 63."

"And... don't leave me hanging!"

"I was having tea with some Jaguar friends of friends at Goodwood in 1966—I think it was 1966 anyway, yes, the last year before all the revival stuff—and one of the blokes mentioned there was a basement in Allesley with a horde of early Jaguar racing parts. I pushed him for more of the story, eventually buying him lunch—and a couple more pints—if he took me there. We arrived at a little brown row house and knocked on the weathered door. An elderly woman—the archetypal old British woman out of Benny Hill—appeared, in a shawl of course. My new mate introduced himself as an old mate of her late son James—they'd worked together in the local fire brigade years before—and she invited us in for tea. While sitting staring at madagascar doilies and framed photographs of the Queen, Princess Di, and the new royal baby—whatever his name was—George asked whether the basement still had old car parts in it.

"She immediately said yes, and that she'd love to get rid of the lot. Taking up room; and she wasn't sure how long she'd be able to get down there anymore any way. George asked if we might have a quick peak. 'By all means luv', she said.

"We ducked our heads and headed down the steep, tiny wooden stairwell, turned the wobbly handle, pushed open the door, and pulled the long dangling string on the one light bulb: I knew immediately how Howard Carter felt. I couldn't make out at first what was all there but I quickly realized it was the parts of these two motorcars sitting right here now. Engines, painted body panels, seats, wheels, everything. And it all looked like new. Thankfully the home's boiler was right next to all the bits, so everything stayed lovely."

"And?" Tanner asked in disbelief.

"I turned to George and asked what in the hell was going on and he said he wasn't sure but the parts may have been saved from the Browns Lane fire back in the fifties. I asked him how he knew and he only let on he'd heard it through the grapevine.

"I didn't want to rip the ol' gal off—who, now come to think of it, was younger than I am today—so I paid her handsomely for everything, and gave George a fist full of quid to keep him quiet about the whole turn of events. And the mum was in heaven as she'd just made plans to pay someone to come and take all the junk away to the dump. Luckily they weren't very reliable: If the binman had only known what he'd missed out on…"

"Now what? Do they have serial numbers?"

"Yes, both do but I've not told anyone about them. I'd just say they're replicas. Not sure how I'm going to pull that off actually. I've only driven them a few miles around my track after putting them back together myself."

"And the E-Type?"

"Well, that's one sad story. A few weeks before a young man went off to Vietnam he married his high school sweetheart and ordered that brand new Jag. He was only 22 and came back six years later than expected as he was a POW. He always remembered there would be a brand new Jag he'd custom-ordered sitting waiting for him: He said that's what kept him going through the hell of it all. When he returned, however, both his wife and the Jaguar were gone. She'd pretty much given up on finding him alive so took the car, and remarried the soldier's best friend. When he returns he's met at the airport by his parents who give him the devastating news. He's obviously beside himself and immediately goes to find them both but they'd been warned of his return and had smartly ran for the hills, and hid the car.

"The car stayed out of sight in her mother's friend's garage in Sedro-Woolley for 30 years until the soldier passed away in a diving accident. The ex wife then finally brought it out into the light of day and a friend of mine, who lived up around there in Concrete who knew the family, called me immediately remembering I was 'into' old cars.

"I couldn't believe my eyes. It was untouched. I mean it was beyond a barn-find, or a time capsule. It looked exactly how it came out of the factory with plastic still on the seats, little paper tags, build marks, everything. I bought it on the spot by giving her far more than she was asking. It's never been washed, touched, or driven on public roads. The odometer shows just 3 miles which, I assume, was factory test mileage. But it's still bittersweet to see it sitting here."

"That's amazing. I would have gunned them down and taken the car back."

"War does strange things Tanner. I know a guy who when he returned from Vietnam could only talk to his Norton Commando for the first six months."

"Let's sit in the XKSS, my leg is bothering me."

"But you'll mess up the dirt."

"Sod the dirt."

"So what are the best, and worst things, about getting elderly?" Tanner asked.

"You mean old? If you mean old, say old."

"You're going to make me say it? OK, so, Mr. Brant, what are the best and worst things about becoming... *vintage*?"

"Hmmm, I like that, *vintage*... OK, best thing is I don't care about what I eat. I used to worry about it all the time. Not that I did much about it mind you but I lost a lot of cycles worrying about it. Now I eat anything I want—including

Devonshire clotted cream, and never gain weight. That's about it."

"You're kidding, really?"

"Yeah, that's about it."

"What about your hard-earned, wisdom?"

"No one cares about it. Well, no one asks about it anyhow. And, frankly, it's probably outdated by now given how fast the world changes."

"Ok, and I'm rather afraid to ask but, what's not so great?"

"If you mean bad, say bad. I'll wait."

"Ok, what's bad? No, what's downright grim?"

"I can't move around easily; can't remember much. And I've been pretty bored much of the time since I turned 60. Up until then it was exciting: new, risky, big wins and losses. Kids all around. Noise. Friends doing crazy new things. Bumping into exotic women. Traveling the world in both high style and low. Meeting the famous, and infamous.

"Then, all of a sudden, Carter was self-sufficient and doing his own thing. Marriages fell apart. I got tired of going to work every day doing the same 'ol same—especially when I realized I had enough dough to not go in anymore; but I was addicted to watching my net worth grow. I allowed myself to believe more cash would provide more opportunities. But I didn't really want any new opportunities. I found myself going to bed before 9, not because I was tired, but because I was bored senseless. The last twenty-something years should have been unbelievable: I had far more money than I could spend. And everything I bought for fun also turned to gold—from real estate, to my automobiles. I've even had so-called trophy-wives all that time—well that's what they call themselves, which is a bit of a tip-off."

"Well that's depressing. What would you have done differently?"

"Just stopped trying to stuff more gold into the bag. Stop worrying so much. Hit the *'I-Don't-Give-a-Shit-itis'* milestone sooner."

"I feel like slitting my throat," Tanner whined. "*'Don't-Give-a-Shit-itis'*, huh?"

"You get to a point in your life that you don't give a shit

anymore. And it comes at a time where you don't really have to give-a-shit about much anyway. You just let stuff not bother you as much. Don't get wound up into everyone else's problems. If you get this early in your life then you need to look out. One only earns this designation once they've lived a full and meaningful life. Anyway, you asked... OK, it's obviously not been that bad. You just caught me on a semi-down day: I'm up and down like a toilet seat. I'll give you a few more in the good column so you don't get blood all over the place: Swimming in the lake with little kids. Eating Mr. Tasty's corn beef hash. Making love to my wife."

"Eww!" Tanner squealed.

"Looking at, driving, and tinkering with my old cars. Learning new things—which is why I've always embraced technology. Years ago I could have easily said it's all too confusing, but I just figure things out through an unbelievable amount of trial and error. The architect world was upset entirely when the drafting board was stolen by the computer. But it allowed me to get a new spark—it was exciting times as the world transitioned to software and their related skills. But the creative parts were still similar, so it was a nice blend. I still love taking photographs—I joined the digital generation years ago when one megapixel cameras were the bee's knees.

"I could never for the life of me understand why so many of my friends and colleagues watched so much television every night, even though no one would admit it. Mostly sports, I guess. I finally figured out why: They had absolutely nothing else to do—night, after night, after night."

"I believe you're right, Mr. Brant. Now it's just TV competing with the internet—and soon they'll be the same thing if they aren't already. What did people do in the 30's?"

"Tried to keep cool in the summer and warm in the winter. And why do you think they all ended up with hordes of children?"

"My dad would come home every night at exactly the same time," Tanner reminisced. "We'd all sit down and eat at precisely 6pm. That rarely happens with our kids these days. And I think we were just as busy back then—mind you, my mum didn't work outside the house. Dad would read the entire paper right after dinner. Circle the kitchen, head to the TV room and only come out for a few more circles of the kitchen. I guess he was happy. Maybe he wasn't? I never asked. And he never said."

"I'm sure he was fine, Tanner. Everyone was doing the same thing. Everyone is basically doing the same thing now, just with different haircuts.

"So to be even a bit more uplifting: Don't worry so much. But that doesn't allow you to be stupid, reckless, or lazy either. As some writer said, *'Don't Sweat the Small Stuff'*, and *'Everything is Small Stuff'*. Easier said than done, trust me. And a loving relationship is critical. Keira and I love each other, I'm fairly sure she does anyway. She has a boy-toy named Quentin—or something like that—I'm not suppose to know about but well, she is over 40 years younger than I. Shoot, she's your age come to think of it! Stay away Mr. Hamilton."

"Well she's certainly hot."

"Hot this, hot that. She's beautiful, stunning, gorgeous. Hot is a temperature not a category of attractiveness."

"Ok, she's beautiful, stunning, and gorgeous. Is that better?"

"No. Stay away or I'll run you over with the half-track.

"And they say exercise is important but I've always followed Neil Armstrong's adage that he was born with a finite number of heartbeats and wasn't about to waste any on exercise. Seemed to have worked well for him anyway—he made it to 82. And walked on the moon. Not bad.

"But then—all of a sudden, out of the blue—something miraculous comes along when you least expect it: like meeting your idol Carroll Shelby, stumbling into a basement with two ultra-rare Jags, being seated by happenstance beside Keira on a plane—or holding your baby granddaughter for the first time. The trick is—now that you've made me really think about it—is to not be so hard on oneself. I'm certainly my own worst critic, biggest enemy in fact. It's weird, isn't it? It's taken me far too many years to allow myself to just 'be': Not accomplish anything. Not beat myself up for neither being productive nor striking something off the never-ending to-do list. Just truly—as the kids say these days—allow myself to kick it. But I guess relaxation for me is boring. Never learned to just sit on the stoop and be content with watching the world go by.

Gregory Long

"And, oh yes, meeting a young man named Tanner has also been therapeutic. Such little surprises keep you going, and smiling."

"Thanks. So, you amassed all this junk I'd never want from architecture?"

"No, from being an architect and a developer. The real money is in being a developer because you can scale that part," Mr. Brant said. "The architect portion is time: lots of time, and exhausting creativity. And working directly with pain-in-the-ass clients who, in some cases, have such a terrible sense of style and proportion, it's maddening. But those issues go away as you get some impressive structures under your belt. And finally you can say, 'If you hire me I get final say even though you're paying the bill.' Obviously it's not that cut and dried but I guess in every profession you have to pay your dues as an underling.

"And I invented something and patented it in the early '70s that you and I, and I believe most people in the world, still use today. Care to guess?"

"Um, an electric toothbrush?"

"Nope. But an impressively dumb guess."

"Electric pencil sharpener?"

"Even dumber, which I thought impossible."

"Shave-cream warming dispenser?"

"What?"

"My dad use to have this contraption that you'd place your can of Barbasol in and it would warm up it up. It was brilliant."

"Nope, and you think everyone around the world uses a shave-cream warming dispenser now?"

"OK, I kind of forgot that part. I give up."

"Luggage wheels."

"You did that?"

"Yes sir—it just came to me. I started by fastening an old roller skate to the bottom of mine as a prototype and everyone in the airport either stared or came over and asked how they could make one. I knew I was onto something, immediately."

"That's truly phenomenal."

"Yes. Yes, it was.

"I also had a smart financial advisor, Daniel, who steered me to diversify my holdings. I preferred to 'go for it' a bit too much and — while he'd still let me dabble — he knew a little less risky route was probably better over the long run, especially with the boom and bust of the real estate world. My biggest personal financial suggestion is if you have options in a company, sell them as they vest. Don't hold too much of your paper net worth in one stock, no matter how bullish you are on it.

"Daniel also understood all these cars here are just another asset category versus others who had no clue and saw them as depreciating assets like normal cars. These automobiles have, amazingly, been one of the — it not the strongest — drivers of my wealth over the years and I didn't even think of them as investments until years after I'd started assembling the group. I find following your heart works pretty well in most cases. Except with wife number two, mind you. But it probably wasn't my heart I was following either."

"So all your cars had to make money for you," Tanner questioned.

"Certainly not. But it was nice when my picks started accelerating in value. I look at it this way: these cars give me enjoyment. Finding them, fixing them, driving them, and meeting others that share like interests. I'd be lying if I said I went in wanting to lose money; but making money wasn't the intent. I see it akin to spending money on travel, taking scuba lessons, eating succulent food at a stellar restaurant — they don't payback financially — but they're still intrinsically valuable. If I end up paying too much for a car, or spending too much on making it roadworthy it's not the end of the world — it's just part of the journey. Buying smartly reduces that risk, somewhat though. And you don't get as much hell from your wife either."

"Well, that's certainly good wisdom. Not outdated at all. Thanks."

"Any cars you wish you'd kept?" Tanner wondered.

"Wish I'd kept the '62 Ferrari California, '19 Kissel Gold Bug Speedster owned by Amelia Earhart..."

"...you don't have her plane around here by any chance do you?" Tanner only partially joked.

"... no but I did try to buy what was purported to be her shoe found on Gardner Island in the South Pacific where her plane supposedly went down... now let's see, a '32 Alfa Romeo 8C 2300 Monza; and I picked up a VW Westfalia Kombi new in Germany in '66. Had it optioned up the wazoo with all the camping stuff including the big tent and the pop-up roof. Went damn slow but we didn't care — we were in absolutely no hurry. Toured all over Europe — down the coast of what was then Yugoslavia — Dubrovnik and Split were unbelievable — into Greece. Parked it for a month in Athens, rented a boat and sailed the Greek Isles. We didn't even know how to sail. Just asked a guy if he'd teach us and, a couple days later, we were off. You learn pretty fast when you have to. Haven't thought about that van, or adventure, for years. Thanks Tanner."

"Colour please."

"You won't believe this but I remember it. I can recall nonsense like that but can't remember my wedding anniversary for the life of me — mind you, I've had three."

"Colour please."

"See, see what I told you?

"Blue white over turquoise."

"L289 over L380, yes, continue," Tanner snuck in.

"It was very attractive. Boy, I wish I still had it. Brought it back on European Delivery but we just didn't use it much; and a neighbor wanted to camp with his little kids so I sold it to him. His name was Victor."

"The neighbour?"

"No, no, the van: Victor the Volkswagen Van. I sure hope he's still trundling along somewhere. I bet he is."

"How I'd love to have it for my family today. I'd trade the Odyssey in a nanosecond! Any more cars? I'm getting greedy now."

"Well let's see... a 1926 Bentley 3 Litre "Red Label" Short Chassis Speed Model. How's that for a mouthful — I always liked saying its name. It's also fun to say, Triumph TR4A IRS. I had a '63 250 GT Lusso that burnt up while spiritedly driving up to Paradise to see Mt. Rainier up close; a '60 250 GT Short Wheel Base Berlinetta Scaglietti I smashed up by stupidly not putting it in gear with the feeble parking brake on; the list goes on... well, actually, not really, I think those are the important ones. Glad I wasn't brain-dead enough to sell the Testa Rossa.

"Oh yeah, a '55 Talbot-Lago T26 Grand Sport and a 1939 Delage D6 Cabriolet. Can't believe I forgot about those two darlings."

"So, Mr. Brant can we check out the motor court and what looks to be an old dealership, or gas station?"

"Sure," Mr. Brant said as he excruciatingly slowly extracted himself from the XKSS and ambled over to the motor court on the north side of the lake.

"Cascadia Court," Tanner read out loud as he spied the old neon sign up high on a white pole.

"Yup, found that sign in Spences Bridge up in BC years ago. And I crazily had these three cottages brought here from near Walla Walla. They were in pretty bad condition so did a bunch of work on them and, well, go in, have a look around. I loved how you used to park your car on the side of your cottage, and close to the lake. Your Country Squire wagon, or perhaps a Plymouth Cranbrook, were an integral part of your family and vacation."

Tanner opened the screen door, then the wooden door, off the front porch to a warm, inviting and bright room with a queen bed staged with too many pillows, a couple side tables, a chrome legged kitchen table and chairs set, and a big comfy couch with a matching floral patterned chair. One of the walls housed a lovely rock fireplace. No TV — just a pack of playing cards.

"Ralph Lauren meets Jackie Gleason is how I like to describe the décor," Mr. Brant said as he stepped in the room.

"Jackie who?"

"Oh, forget it."

"Where's the washroom? And is there wireless," Tanner said knowing Mr. Brant's certain reaction.

"No gosh darn wireless. You're getting on my goat!"

"Getting on my goat? Isn't it *Get my goat*?" Tanner poked.

"I don't know. It's an idiomatic phrase I suppose... numbskull."

"Where's the washroom?"

"Washroom? We call it a bathroom in this country."

"But what if there's no bath in the bathroom? Is it then referred to as a shower-room?"

"Oh God help me. The WC is over in the dealership."

"Our next stop, I hope," Tanner quipped.

"Sure. I've got to pee anyway."

With that they walked back outside and towards the brick building with a couple of old forties Chevron gas pumps out front under a large portico.

"I remember those garbage cans, Mr. Brant," Tanner said excitedly. "I can't believe you have one—I haven't seen one in years."

"I guess they got rid of them because they didn't keep the bears out. Carter use to love to put garbage in the beaver's mouth. I think they were called Garbage Gobblers."

"Is it a beaver? Looks more like a demented frog to me," Tanner responded. "But I did love them too—they were all up and down the highways as I recall. It was the only time we'd all fight to put the trash in the garbage. Perhaps I should get one for our house?" Tanner said, thinking perhaps he'd found his first entrepreneurial enterprise.

"Open those shutters if you would please," Mr. Brant said as they arrived at the old gas station/dealership. As Tanner swung and collapsed the huge shutters into each other he noticed on the other side of the huge plate glass windows stood a Speedster and a 550.

"This is my interpretation of what a Porsche dealership might have looked like in a relatively small American city in the mid-to-late fifties. Nothing fancy. Not spick and span, or dirty for that matter, but enthusiast owned—a place where guys stood around and bullshitted about racing, and women."

"These cars must have stories, right Mr. Brant?"

"That 550 is a kit car actually. I wanted something I could just drive and not worry about. I bought it from a guy on eBay who'd had all the parts in his garage but never got around to assembling it. It was actually rather fun—using all new parts is pretty exciting after restoring so many old cars over the years."

"You mean 'resurrecting' don't you, Mr. Brant?"

"No, I've mostly been restoring all my life. We didn't accept them screwed-up back then. They all needed to gleam like new. But most of the cars I restored over the years weren't good enough to preserve anyway. Or that's what I keep telling myself.

"I put a nice bored-out VW engine in it and it goes like stink."

"And the Speedster's a replica too?"

"Nope, it's the real McCoy. Check the rear hatch."

"A Speedster Carrera? Don't tell me that's a 4 cam!"

"Yes, its full moniker is a 1956 356 Carrera GS/GT Speedster. I bought it years ago when it had a pushrod motor. I didn't really care at the time as I didn't plan on racing it; and had heard such horror stories about the 4 cam engines. But then, as I got older and had a few more bucks, it was really important to me I find and install a proper engine. They've always been as rare as hen's teeth so it took me years to find one, eventually paying far more for the engine than I had for the car. It was rebuilt by one of a handful of guys that can do it, properly. Engine was installed in the car. It drove wonderfully. All was good.

"Until I got a call from a guy who purportedly had the original numbers-matching engine for it. And we all know how frothy everyone gets over matching-numbers—especially in the Corvette world but it's everywhere now. The seller knew he had me over a barrel. He said he got it out of an old oval beetle behind an ice cream burger joint somewhere. Obviously a numbers-matching car is worth far more—he held the magic key. We eventually arrived at a number that didn't make me sweat too much, and made him over-the-moon ecstatic.

"So I've got a spare 4 cam engine now sitting over there—I'm just waiting for the Porsche to appear that it goes with," Mr. Brant said with a devious smile. "I should be able to recoup some of that crazy money."

"You say 'Por-sha' not Porsh."

"I guess I do."

"Don't you feel a little pretentious saying it that way? At least here in the States where most say Porsh?"

"The unwashed masses say Porsh. They say Porsh because they don't know how to say it properly. I also hate Renalt when it's Ren-oh. Citroën as Sit-tron. I could go on. But, yes, I am pretentious by the way. I was an architect in the '60s and you *had* to be pretentious to get work.

"And I still have to pee," Mr. Brant said in a more strained voice. "Come have a look at the bathrooms, I mean, washrooms, whatever…"

Mr. Brant and Tanner walked to the side of the garage where two porcelain signs stuck out above two doors: Men and Ladies.

"Open the women's one Tanner. I hope it's the first time you've been in one," Mr. Brant joked as he wiggled his ears.

"Did you just, wiggle your ears, Mr. Brant?"

"Yes, can't everyone? And can you tuck your earlobes in your ears so they stay like this too?"

"Nope. And nope. You must be a real card at parties."

"It gets them every time, especially the little ones."

Tanner walked into the Ladies and was flabbergasted to step into what seemed like a gorgeous dream bathroom at the *Four Seasons*: A huge tub overlooked the Pacific far below; shelves chock-full of expensive-looking potions. Insanely thick fluffy white towels, with matching dressing gowns embroidered with little racecars, hung at the ready.

"I was a bit worried my female guests wouldn't find the quaint retro cottages as enticing as I did so I splurged on their bathroom facilities. I love how it shocks everyone. Check out the Men's."

With that Tanner opened the little creaky door with the silhouette of a man and was met with exactly what he'd expected to see: An old porcelain pedestal sink with separate hot and cold faucets, a mirror with an ancient torn ESSO sticker on it, and a long chrome pump for soap. A toilet, and a big white subway tile shower with a plastic shower curtain with racecars on it completed the scene. And, or course, a proper urinal.

"Now, get out. I've got to relieve myself—and this could take awhile."

"Well, try to remember this then, Mr. Brant:

'When water hits water it makes a sound all can hear.
'When water hits porcelain it falls softly to the ear.'"

"I plan on using the urinal," Mr. Brant yelled back.

"I know, I just wanted to recite that poem to prove how dazzling and deep my vast intellect is."

"Nice Muskoka chairs," Tanner mentioned as they ambled over to a couple of weather-beaten 'Martha Stewart'esque blue' chairs on the dock.

"Muskoka? No, they're Adirondack chairs; remember we're in the States."

"Tomato. Tomahto," Tanner said with a smirk.

"So son, what are your plans for the future? Doesn't sound like the newspaper business pumps through your veins. You haven't mentioned it once."

"It's a job. Puts food on the table and all that. I fell into it, it's OK money and, well, there's not a lot around here that excites me. It's funny you should ask though. I was out driving the other day listening to NPR when a segment on singer-songwriter Guy Clark came on. I'd never heard of him, you?"

"Yes sir, he's a West Texan. I don't think he's ever had a big commercial success but I have a feeling he couldn't care less either. If you really listen to his lyrics, he's just doing what he loves," Mr. Brant said.

"Yes, he did sound like an interesting soul in that interview. Lyrics, he said, should never spell out the entire story. The listener needs to figure out what they mean, to them. He said he still can't listen to one of his songs without rewriting 'this or that' part in his head. Forever editing. A work in progress, he said.

Gregory Long

"And one of his songs gave me my second musical epiphany. The first came over 15 years ago with U2's *"I Still Haven't Found What I'm Looking For"* — which steered me to the love of my life. I'm getting pretty sappy, aren't I?"

"Yes, but go on. Sappy is underrated. What song?"

"*Boats to Build*. I just thought, at first, he was singing about building a boat. That's nice. Something both worthwhile and fun. But it wasn't about building anything. Except, it turns out, my own next chapter."

Mr. Brant jumped in, "I love that song. Go back and grab my old Martin over there in the garage, if you would."

"This is gorgeous, I'm sure it has a story too."

"Course. It was Neil's."

"As in Young?"

"Yes, he'd left this guitar to be fixed for some reason at a shop on Sunset Boulevard and when he came back the entire store had disappeared. Nothing left, including his guitar.

"I'd got it a few years later from a guy who owed me money for something or other — can't for the life of me remember what. I didn't believe his story till I saw a photo of Neil holding that exact guitar playing at Massey Hall in Toronto in '71: Same exact discoloration as right here, see? It's a D41. Neil wrote an autobiography recently and in it he told the same story of losing his guitar when a music store closed down. I wrote a letter to his manager advising him I had it if they wanted it returned. Happily, I never heard back. So I've got good karma from coming clean and telling them, and even better karma because I get to play it guilt-free!"

"So this is the actual guitar you hear Neil playing on his ground-breaking *Live at Massey Hall* album?"

"All indications say yes.

"I've got another couple in my den I've collected over the years: *The Les Paul* Eric Clapton played as lead on the *White Album's While My Guitar Gently Weeps*, and a '58 Rickenbacker 325 Lennon used a lot early-on in both the studio and onstage. The one I probably shouldn't have sold was the Strat Seattleite Jimi Hendrix played the *Star Spangled Banner* on at Woodstock: Paul Allen of Microsoft fame just offered me far too much money for it. It's now at the EMP where all can soak up its mystical aura, so that's OK."

"Please stop. I can't take this anymore, really. I'm a mere mortal... and Clapton played lead on a Beatles album? I thought that was a Harrison song?"

"It was but George wanted Eric to play it."

"So do you have Babe Ruth's bat around here somewhere — the one he was holding when he pointed out to the grandstands and hit a homer?"

"Yes, I think it's holding up some of Keira's tomato plants out in the garden."

"I don't play anywhere near as well as my son Carter but let's get really sappy!" Mr. Brant said as he tuned up and they sang, together:

> *It's time for a change*
> *I'm tired of that same ol' same*
> *The same ol' words the same ol' lines*
> *The same ol' tricks and the same ol' rhymes*
>
> ...

"We should start a boy band, whaddya think?" Tanner laughed. '*Tanner and the Old Guy'.*"

"Hardly. '*The Distinguished Gentleman and the Van Driving Punk*', don't you mean? So what's this second epiphany you had?"

"Well, *Boats to Build* gave me approval and — as my mom would have said — a good swift kick, to move on to something new. Not necessarily tomorrow, or next month but sooner than I've ever allowed myself to think about before. Uncharted waters, so to speak, get it? Life's too short and all that. And Paige is in full support."

"Well that's certainly as good a segue as any: You definitely know your car stuff and, frankly, after spending far too much time with you I have to say, sincerely, you are an amazing young man. You are a true joy to be with, have your head on straight, care deeply about your girls — all three of them — have a great sense of humor and, most importantly, you've got your car colors down pat, so I have a proposal for you — and this isn't a full-time gig mind you but it might just help you steer your boat towards where we both know you should head: Your passion for old, wonderful automobiles. Doing a job everyday you love, isn't really a job.

"So, how about you help me sell them on, the vast majority anyway? I want to keep a few for Carter, my grandkids and, of course, myself, but I really need to cull the herd. I'm obviously not getting any healthier. And while it'll surely be difficult to let them go I'd rather be involved in all the excitement with the new owners—showing the photos of gorgeous Pinky picking up her new Chapron at the factory in Paris, the eType as it sat in the bright sun on the lawn outside the garage it spent decades in, to shocking the world with McQueen's Mustang, and Sean's Aston Martin. Boy, wouldn't that be fun! It's all about passing down the stories.

"I've thought of having an auction right here—maybe letting qualified folks drive the cars around my track for big money before the auction with all proceeds going to charity; or maybe taking them all to Pebble Beach, or somewhere? Not sure. But that's what I'd like you to figure out, Tanner. I'll give you $25,000 up-front and half a percent of the net proceeds for getting them all ready, managing the entire affair—and handing me a Kleenex each time one gets hammered down. Half a percent might not sound like much but, trust me, selling that Testa Rossa should bring you a tidy sum all by itself."

Tanner didn't have time to even remotely figure out what his take might be before blurting out, "Of course! Yes, I'd love to!... and I guess that means I might have to drive them a little bit too, right?"

"Of course, let's celebrate right now. Pick anyone you want, and you drive."

Now... kindly flip the page for the awe-inspiring FOUND game!

Found / FoundCarsOfCascadia.com

Gregory Long

1970 BMW 2800 CS Coupe	Ferry Porsche
1967 Saab Sonett II	William Lyons
1957 Ferrari 250 Testa Rossa	Giulio Alfieri
1967 Citroën DS 21 Chapron	René Bonnet
1967 Jaguar XK-E FHC	Alec Issigonis
1974 Land Rover Series III	Lee Iacocca
1957 Mercedes Benz 300SL	Henri Chapron
1971 Plymouth Barracuda	David Dunbar Buick
1967 Panhard 24BT	Max Hoffman
1968 Buick Wildcat	David Brown
1967 BMC Mini Moke	Jean Panhard
2001 Saab 9-3 Viggen	André Lefèbvre
1934 Citroën 22CV	Adolphe Kégresse
1957 Maserati 200Si	Hawley Bowlus
1935 Bowlus Road Chief	Wilhelm Hofmeister
1994 Morgan Plus 8	John Herlitz
1956 Citroën DS19	Henry Morgan
1957 Jaguar D-Type	Preston Tucker
1953 Jaguar XK120	Eric Carlsson
1961 Alfa Giulietta Sprint Zagato	Paul Magès
1967 Toyota 2000GT	Björn Karlström
1935 Tatra T77a	Ugo Zagato
1956 Volkswagen Beetle	Maurice Wilks
1948 Tucker Torpedo	Lofty England
1953 Chevrolet Corvette	Gordon Murray
1965 Shelby Cobra 289	Hans Ledwinka
1965 Amphicar 770	Satoru Nozaki
1994 McLaren F1	Zora Arkus-Duntov
1973 Ferrari Dino 246 GTS	Carroll Shelby
1973 Citroën SM	Enzo Ferrari
1967 Porsche 911S Targa	Hanns Trippel
2013 Tesla Model S	André Citroën
1934 Citroën Half-Track	Ferdinand Porsche
1964 Citroën 2CV AZAM	Alfredo Ferrari
1968 Ford Mustang GT 390 Fastback	Butzi Porsche
1964 Aston Martin DB5	Elon Musk
1956 Deutsch Bonnet Super Rallye	Robert Opron
1966 Volkswagen Westfalia Kombi	Malcolm Sayer
1956 Porsche 356 Speedster	Ben Pon

Answer Key:

Now kindly go to this book's companion site at FoundCarsOfCascadia.com — yes, this was a trick to incentivise you to:

- Read more about these interesting cars, including a *'Author's Cut'* on how I came up with many of the cars and their stories

- Additional photos of the cars

- Read great input from readers like you — share your car stories and photographs; and, yes,

- To view the *Answer Key*!

Gregory Long

Found / FoundCarsOfCascadia.com

Made in the USA
Middletown, DE
19 May 2015